Teachi  lf

Teaching Arabs, Writing Self

Memoirs of an Arab-American Woman

Evelyn Shakir

OLIVE
BRANCH
PRESS

An imprint of Interlink Publishing Group, Inc.
www.interlinkbooks.com

First published in 2014 by

OLIVE BRANCH PRESS
An imprint of Interlink Publishing Group, Inc.
46 Crosby Street, Northampton, Massachusetts 01060
www.interlinkbooks.com

Library of Congress Cataloging-in-Publication Data

Shakir, Evelyn, 1938-
Teaching Arabs, writing self : memoirs of an American woman / by Evelyn Shakir.
pages cm
ISBN 978-1-56656-924-8
1. Shakir, Evelyn, 1938- 2. Shakir, Evelyn, 1938---Travel--Middle East. 3. English
teachers--Middle East--Biography. 4. Lebanese American women--Massachusetts--
Biography. 5. Lebanese Americans--Massachusetts--Biography. I. Title.
PE64.S43A3 2013
818'.603--dc23
[B]
2013023656

General Editor: Michel Moushabeck
Copyeditor: Kitty Florey
Proofreader: Jennifer M. Staltare
Cover and book design: Pam Fontes-May

Printed and bound in the United States of America

10 9 8 7 6 5 4 3 2 1

To request our complete 48-page, full-color catalog, please call us toll free at 1-800-
238-LINK, visit our website at www.interlinkbooks.com, or send us an e-mail:
info@interlinkbooks.com

To
My father, Wadie
My mother, Hannah
My brother, Philip
Iconoclasts all

Shakir Hannah philip Wadie Josphine
Juliet and Evelyn Shakir
Bowdoin college 1956

Contents

Preface

In recent years, I have taught American literature to university students in three Arab countries: Lebanon, Syria, and the archipelago kingdom of Bahrain. In Damascus a man asked me how I liked my students. "Very much," I said. "I learn from them every day."

He shook his head in protest. "The eye," he said, calling on an Arab proverb, "does not sit above the eyebrow."

Despite his gallantry, he was, of course, mistaken. I did learn— how could I not?—from my students as well as from other Syrians, whether friends, shopkeepers, or cabbies. In Lebanon and Bahrain, it was the same.

This two-way street, my teaching others, their teaching me, is reflected in the title of my book. Just as "hanging judges" hang and "kissing cousins" kiss, "teaching Arabs" may teach; think of those pictures where, if you stare at them long enough, foreground and background swap around. The second half of the title performs a similar do-si-do: "self" both the writer and the written about. And, of course, "self" and "Arab" have been brought under a single roof for a reason. Cohabitation implies intimate connection.

Because what took me to Arab lands, initially, was a belated desire to connect with my own heritage. As a child of immigrants from

Lebanon, I had tried to run from it. My goal was to be "American," and to expunge in myself every trace of foreignness. In those days before we'd wrapped our tongues around "multiculturalism" and "diversity," our teachers, the news media, politicians, and pop culture all conspired to promote ethnic amnesia and urge assimilation. I was a good student; I bought it all. If there was a flaw in their definition of "American," I couldn't see it. I think the closest I came to suspecting something was amiss was when I would mention the name of one classmate or another to my parents. "Oh," they would say—like pulling a rabbit out of a hat—"he's Italian" or "she's Irish" or "he's Greek." I began to wonder: "So who are the *Americans* and where are *they* hanging out?" It took years before I could say, with Pogo-like certainty, "I have met the Americans and they are us."

Given that personal history, it has made sense to me to divide this book into three sections: one that reflects on my early attempts to sort out my identity (and related family matters); one that explores my teaching abroad; and, finally, one that looks inward again but at a different hour and under a different sky.

I
Childhood

Evelyn's graduation from Wellesley College

At Home and Away:
Thirteen Takes on Growing Up Arab in America

1

It's my experience that Arabs and psychiatrists are natural enemies. One says, "Family first." The other says, "Only neurotics call home every day." Another difference is that Arabs don't want to hear a word about psychiatry. It hurts their ears. "Ooft," they say. "What's this craziness!" But psychiatrists are eager to pry into Arab psyches—expecting to find a house of horrors. Each group calls the other bonkers.

My mother and father were immigrants from Lebanon. I was born in the United States. In the eighties, when Americans were being kidnapped in Beirut, a therapist explained to me the source of my unhappiness: "Your family is holding you hostage," she said. She was being clever. She was pleased with herself.

2

My Uncle Yusuf, a gentle man, loved America but hated Catholics, Democrats, and Jews. Mention the pope to him, he'd come close to spitting. Jews, of course, were the usurpers, planting themselves on Arab land. Which also explained his venom toward Democrats and Harry Truman, in particular, who'd waited all of 11 minutes before saying *yes* when Jews in Palestine declared themselves a state.

My Uncle Yusuf loved his suburban garden. He grew vegetables for his wife, and flowers for the joy of it. Flashy blooms—dahlias, giant chrysanthemums, and ruffled peonies. He cradled their heads in his huge hands. He cooed to them like a lover. Their enemies were his enemies. He picked off Japanese beetles with his bare fingers and drowned them in a can of kerosene. He called them "Trumans."

My Uncle Yusuf loved me. One day, when it was just the two of us in his car, he asked the standard question. "What do you want to be when you grow up?" To be funny, I said, "President." He said, "Why not?" A window in my mind flew open. I began to think things I'd never thought before.

3

To American diplomats who urged Truman to hold off on recognizing Israel, he cited the wishes of American Jews: "I am sorry, gentlemen, but I have to answer to hundreds of thousands who are anxious for the success of Zionism: I do not have hundreds of thousands of Arabs among my constituents."

On a Christmas show, back in the fifties, Perry Como croons carols on TV but also works in Jewish folk songs. My father, passing through the living room, overhears. "Jews!" he explodes. "Do they control everything?" I go into my bedroom and slam the door. Only years after he died did I begin to understand what it felt like for my father to be an Arab in the United States, reminded in every editorial, on every channel, that on matters that mattered, he could have no political voice.

Good that he didn't live to see '67 and Israel's six-day blitzkrieg against Syria and Egypt, when newsmen and even comics on American TV gloated openly at Israel's victory, when Arabs were mocked pitilessly.

4

The early seventies. Palestinians are hijacking airliners and planting bombs. After one horrific attack, I'm on a bus, riding through a Boston neighborhood where Syrians and Lebanese have lived for decades. An old man climbs on. He is drunk and disheveled. "Oh, Arabs," he cries out in Arabic, swaying from one overhead strap to another. His tears spill. "Oh, brothers, what have you done!" The driver, who has understood nothing, mutters an ethnic epithet and puts him off the bus.

5

My father's best fishing buddy was Mr. Rosenfield who sold silk ties and held his pants up with suspenders. Before dawn on a Saturday, his black Pontiac would drive down our street, and my father, who'd been at the window watching for headlights, would flick off the porch light and be out the door. Gear loaded, the two were off for the day, out after white perch and striped bass—freshwater fish. Forget the sea. Cape Cod had 365 bodies of water, my father claimed, a new one for each day of the year. When they arrived at their special spot, the sun just rising, the morning mist still on the lake, they spread out along the shore in opposite directions. Mirror images. Clumsy figures in waist-high fishermen's boots, wading cautiously into water. Product of shtetl or mountain, neither man knew how to swim. But they knew rule number one: don't talk, don't call out, don't scare the fish.

At noon, under a fringe of trees, they unrolled a patchwork blanket of wool remnants my mother had pieced together on her sewing machine. Pulled out sandwiches wrapped in wax paper (fried eggplant for my father, something that smelled of fish for Mr. Rosenfield), hard-boiled eggs, whole tomatoes they bit into like apples, thermoses of sweetened black coffee, cinnamon buns picked up the day before from a favorite bakery. Afterwards, my father puffing on his pipe, Mr. Rosenfield on his cigarette, they relaxed into conversation. What did they talk about then, this Arab and this Jew? Rods and reels, maybe. Lures and live bait. Irish politicians.

6

Riding the bus to work or waiting for the fish to bite, my father must often have dreamed of home. That would be Zahle, a good-sized town in a fertile patch of Lebanon set down between two mountain ranges. Born in the 1880s, an émigré by 1901, he thought well all his life of anybody—himself included—who had roots there. It went beyond a natural attachment. As late as 1960, an historian could write that people from Zahle "exhibit an intense, almost fanatic pride in family, status, and in place of origin." It drove my mother crazy: "These men from Zahle, who do they think they are!"

The Zahlawi, explained the historian, has a personal relationship with God and with the saints, whom he approaches "as he would an equal." That sounded right to me. America might snub them, hold them of no account, but it never occurred to my father, my uncle, and their cousins that they were not in excellent standing with the Almighty.

Standing among their own kind mattered, too. The Zahlawi men I knew demanded respect and were quick to take offense. ("She asked me how many eggs did I want for breakfast," my uncle Jiryes sputtered. "I was a guest in her house, and she was counting eggs.") Like boys in the 'hood, they thought rep was everything. In the old country, their ancestors—those they chose to remember, those whose framed photos hung over the divan—had been *abaday* who galloped through town and down hillside, ready for battle should anyone dis them or their clan. But honor also demanded that, however much or little they had, Zahlawis give without stint to kinsmen, guests, and others under their protection. In America, the sons still harbored that obsession. The grandiose gesture was what they lived by; the open hand was their family crest. When the offering plate came round, heavy with coins, they tossed in dollar bills. When wedding invitations arrived, they didn't stoop to Mixmasters or pressure cookers. Hand-embroidered linens were more their style; brass trays from Tripoli, designs hammered by master craftsmen; end tables from Damascus, inlaid with rosewood, olivewood, and alabaster.

My father ran a one-man printing press, turning out invoices, stationery, ad books, and volumes of Arabic poetry. It was the poetry he cared about. Which may be why he never got ahead. But he handed out what he could, basins of tomatoes and string beans and blackberries from his garden. In the coffee shop, he slapped away any hand that reached for the check.

Recently in Boston a young Lebanese cabbie picked me up at the airport. It turned out he was from Zahle and thrilled that I had connections there, too. I told him my father's surname. "A small family," he said, "but respectable." I told him my grandmother's maiden name. "A very good family," he said. At my door, he made the grand gesture. "Auntie, pay whatever you wish." If I'd played by the rules of his game, he would have made out like a bandit and I would have walked into my house a princess, a queen. When I fell short, he shook his head sadly. Did he write home about me? Did he send word: "In America, how the children of the Zahlawi are fallen!"

My brother saw the advantage in keeping to the old ways. As a little boy, he refused to help weed the garden. "It's below my dignity," he explained. That's when my mother knew, to her frustration, that her son was more Zahlawi than her husband. Physical labor, a necessity for most immigrants in America but among the *abaday* in Zahle a source of shame. "A Zahlawi," one of their own has said, "is so proud that, if he bought something and it had to be put in a bag, he would hire a servant to carry it."

But when I needed a typewriter for college, my father found one downtown and lugged it home after work, on the subway and then on the bus and then down the street to our house. Though by then he was 70. "No," I said after I'd pecked out a few letters. "I want larger type."

7

My parents could not get anything right:

Couldn't talk right. *Beoble*, they sometimes said when tired, stymied by the letter *p*. Or else they overcompensated. Car *pumper*.

Couldn't eat right: okra, eggplant, bulgur, and yogurt—my mother made her own. Bread with pockets. Hummus and tabouli. "Don't put that stuff in my lunch box," I said.

Went to the wrong church. Not Catholic, not Protestant, not even Jewish. "Huh?" the kids said when I said, "Orthodox."

Were too old. One parent over 40 when I was born, the other over 50. "Is this your granddaughter?" the saleslady said.

Smoked, drank. Miss Young, my fifth grade teacher, said those were things the better class of people didn't do.

Were eccentric. My father had a bald head and a Groucho mustache that strangers stared at. And an inch-long nail on the little finger of one hand—back home, a sign of aristocracy. My mother, odd in her own way, had a job. Miss Young said that was wrong for a married lady. And then it got worse. In April that year, my mother rented a storefront a quarter mile from school and installed two banks of sewing machines, some Singer, some Wilcox and Gibbs, all second-hand. She was going into business for herself, just like a man.

8

Equipment in place, my mother looked to manufacturers downtown who would contract work to her. The earliest and steadiest source was Mr. Lerner, whose clothing line was "Debbie Lu," his daughter's name. "Jews are like us," my mother said. "They love their children." Every so often, on his way home from the city, Mr. Lerner dropped by our house. My mother, flustered by the novelty of a guest who wasn't family, directed him to the best chair in the parlor and brought out the Canadian Club, offering it neat or with a splash of water. But, as she knew, he was there on business. A new style of bathrobe or of pedal pushers to be laid out on the coffee table and its price haggled over. My mother would hold out her arms for the sample, exposing scars that ran across both palms and several inches up her wrists. Four times while I was still in public school, or maybe five, she disappeared into the hospital where doctors cut away ganglion cysts the size of eggs. Each time, propped up in bed, she'd hold a pre-operative conference with the surgeon, offering her professional opinion. Figuring she knew at least as much as he did about where to cut and how to stitch.

With the sample garment turned inside out and back again, she would tick off what it required by way of zipper, pockets, darts, or lining. A lot of work, she'd finally say. She didn't know: could she turn a profit? She had left Lebanon at 12, manned textile looms at 14, and been a worker all her life. Now she was a boss and desperate to succeed. Mr. Lerner would set down his glass and rub his knees. "Look at it my way, Missus. I also have to eat." Eventually, they'd agree on maybe 15 more cents per garment; only time would tell if she'd been outmaneuvered. For now, courtesy dictated that she bring out her fancy sweets and brew a pot of coffee.

Later, in her shop, she'd go through the same dance with her workers.

"A lot to this new style," they'd say. "It's complicated. Setting in this collar will be tricky."

"Seven more cents."

"That's all?"

"Ladies, look at it my way."

9

Midway between my mother's factory and my grammar school stood Washington Boulevard Methodist Church, where regular Americans went on Sunday. I was 12 the first time I walked in, invited by my best friend, Ruth, a tall, pale girl whose father was superintendent of the Sunday School. In my pink cotton gloves and new straw hat, I sat beside her, waiting for the preliminaries to conclude and church to start, until it came to me that it was already underway. This casual get-together of civilians.

I'd been expecting something like the rituals of Saint George's Orthodox Church, where my family attended Easter services. Had been waiting for priests to appear, in embroidered stoles and colorful robes down to their ankles, swinging censers that lofted clouds of incense, chanting prayers in a foreign language, sing-songing scripture. The whole performance as stylized and impenetrable as the Metropolitan operas my brother tuned in to on Saturday afternoon. Instead I got a white-haired gentleman in a business suit who threw one arm across a lectern and talked straight at us, attacking some government proposal that was in the news. He might as well have been a neighbor dropped by to pass the time and argue politics. A man as ordinary as his church windows with their clear panes that looked out on privet hedges and were open now to catch the morning breeze. An intercourse with the world that seemed almost sacrilegious.

It was this confusion of inside and outside, sacred and secular, that baffled me at first. But, as I came back with Ruth, week after week, I grew to like the way Methodists went about things. It was clean and free of foreign quirkiness.

And it was orderly. Not like the interminable Orthodox services, where people came and went as they pleased, arriving late, leaving early, or cutting out for a cigarette. The service might be scripted to a fare-thee-well, but the parishioners were not. Instead of sitting quietly in place, the Orthodox of that day were just as apt to mill around, pew-hopping to say hello to friends. Or, if they were men of a certain stripe, crowding to the front, close to the altar and the action, and then just standing there, exercising male prerogative. One thing no one did was sit with legs crossed—something about the crucifixion. That aside, they were mostly uninhibited. I remember a tiny old woman in black, a pew to herself, sobbing into her open hands.

At Washington Boulevard, it was the other way around. The minister was spontaneous, the congregation decorous. These were people like Ruth's family, who knew how to behave and would never raise their voices or humiliate their children. They stood to sing hymns and to recite the Apostle's Creed, but otherwise kept to their role as audience, mannerly and attentive. Even when they took communion, they didn't have to stir. Tiny cubes of bread and thimbles of grape juice were passed around on trays, like sugar cookies and tea in somebody's front parlor. At St. George, communicants made their way out pew and down aisle to a priest, chalice in hand, who spoon fed them bread crumbled in wine. At the end of the service, they filed by again, kissing a cross he held out to them, and then helping themselves to chunks of consecrated bread. Something to stanch their hunger on the ride home.

10

Two times that I remember, Gloria sang the female lead in our school's annual operetta—Gretel one year, the next year Martha. At Washington Boulevard, her soprano carried the Sunday choir. Blond and petite, she was just old enough—five years my senior—to make me her project. She gave me the first book of poetry I'd ever owned, Frost's *North of Boston*; introduced me to Handel's *Messiah*; and, on summer afternoons, had me over to her house, where we sat under a pear tree with tall glasses of her mother's fresh-squeezed lemonade. It was pretty there—yellow tea roses, masses of tiger lilies, bronze butterflies visiting blossoms of white summersweet. I don't remember much conversation. Just Gloria, sunlight in her hair, reading her favorite poems to me. And me listening as hard as I knew how.

I remember too one particular Sunday. The day before, there'd been a gathering of outsiders in the church hall, a club meeting or perhaps a luncheon. In any case, they hadn't picked up all their trash. Gloria caught me on my way into church and filled me in, then took me by the elbow. "You know," she whispered, "we just shouldn't rent to Lebanese and Syrians."

11

One year, my family had an important visitor from overseas, a second cousin, who brought us a framed photo of himself, with medals and a sash across his chest. Forever after, that photo stared out at us from a low table in the living room. On the Sunday morning he was with us in the flesh, everyone prepared for church, which meant St. George's, my parents probably pretending that this was something they did every week. "Come with us," my mother coaxed me. But I held my ground. By then I was a confirmed member of the Methodist church and that's where I was headed. I didn't want any black marks against my soul.

When the cousin found out what was going on, he made a joke. "I wouldn't mind," he said, "if it were a real religion." Of course, he was arrogant, and, of course, I was offended. But I was also startled, as if a giant hand had picked me up and set me down again, facing in the opposite direction. I was used to (or had assumed) Protestant disdain for Eastern churches and, by extension, for the East itself. But apparently it was possible to turn the tables. To look at my American-style church and dismiss it as a hollow imitation of a faith that had the weight of many centuries behind it. *Superior* and *inferior* were terms capable of changing place. And if Protestantism could be called into question, why not this Protestant nation itself, its politics, its culture? It would be a lie to say such reasoning ran through my mind that Sunday morning. But something took hold. An inkling that there might be treasures I had turned my back on. That I might not always have to be ashamed.

12

From my childhood, I remember postcards that came in the mail, with Arabic writing on the back and stamps featuring some beefy man with abundant whiskers and a fez. "Zahle," my father would say, pointing to the gray or sepia photograph on the front, caressing it with his thumb. Just home from work, he'd hold it under a table lamp or, in summer, take it to the kitchen window. Silhouetted against the late afternoon light, a man in his fifties, then sixties, then seventies, each year his back more stooped from hours hunched over a printing press, his round eyes watery from tweezing characters out of a box and setting each page of text by hand. With the photo tilted this way, then that, he'd shift his glasses to study it more closely. What was he looking for in its shadows? What had he lost?

At 16, my father had come to America; at 75, he died without seeing home again, the postcards as close as he came. Even as a child,

I knew that slump of flat-roofed houses squatting on a hillside meant the world to him. But my idea of pretty was yellow flowers, green grass, and white clapboard houses on streets shaded with sugar maples. In the morning, my mother went to a factory, my father to his press. The New Deal Press he called it in honor of the patrician president who cared about the little man. Meanwhile, I was off to school, where I grew up with Dick and Jane. But, more than the storybook words, it was the sun-washed illustrations that taught me what was beautiful and right—Mother at the door in a checked gingham apron waving good-bye to Father who wore a fedora and carried a briefcase; blue-eyed Baby Sally gurgling in her crib; and, best place in the world, Grandmother and Grandfather's farm, with golden haystacks, snow-white lambs.

For years, when grownups asked me, "Wouldn't you like to visit the old country?" I'd remember my father's dismal postcards and say no.

13

On my first trip to Lebanon I changed planes in Paris. At Orly, I was already seated and strapped in when passengers were instructed to disembark. In the afternoon sun, our luggage had been lined up on the tarmac, and each of us stepped forward to identify our bags. Then we were herded back on board.

I trooped on with the others although I knew the plane was going to crash. Disaster, mayhem—how had I forgotten? This was what the Middle East was all about. I'd wanted this trip for the adventure and to see my parents' homeland. Times had changed. Black was beautiful, exotic was in, the melting pot was yesterday's thinking. But I'd been apprehensive from the start and met with a psychiatrist to talk it out. He didn't understand. Four hours from Paris to Beirut; I figured the bomb was scheduled to explode midway.

The next morning, I sat on the terrace of the Hotel Melkart—

named after the ancient King of the Underworld and Protector of the Universe—drinking in the scents of jasmine and white gardenia, nursing a demitasse of sweet Turkish coffee. In the distance ahead, gulls rode the sea breezes like a roller coaster; below them, in a dazzle of sunlight, the blue-green Mediterranean kept on to the horizon.

Ghost ships passed, silhouetted against the pale sky. High-prowed Phoenician vessels, plowing their way from Byblos, Beirut, Tyre, Sidon. Voyaging to North Africa, on through the Straits, into open, unknown waters. And steamships, traveling in their wake, carrying my parents and my grandparents.

Later in the morning, I would find a driver to take me to my mother's village, where my aunt was waiting (and, on another day, inland to Zahle). "You are going home": my mother had said it like a promise. Time would tell, I thought. For now, it was enough to have leapt borders and landed safely. To perch for this half hour on this threshold. Anonymous. Unclaimed. And hostage only to my own imaginings.

I have seldom been so content.

Members of the Syrian Ladies' Aid Society of Boston
preparing to march in the Armistice Day parade of 1925

Mother

A few years before my mother was born, with the fever to emigrate already spreading like contagion through Mount Lebanon, her father, Jiryes, stowed away on a ship bound for "America." To his astonishment, it deposited him in Brazil. That adventure hadn't worked out as expected, but within a few years of his return he was ready to try again. This time accompanied by his two oldest sons, now of an age to participate in the enterprise and able to speak a rudimentary English they'd picked up in school, Jiryes made it to his intended destination, Massachusetts. A third son followed, and, once the three brothers had found steady work and a flat (or maybe just a rented room), Jiryes returned. Beachhead established.

Up next was his wife, Miriam. What was this America all about? With Jiryes left behind to tend to the younger children, and a sister-in-law to help him out, Miriam sailed away to her sons in Boston. It was a year before she returned home. And perhaps another year or two before she and Jiryes made that leap of the imagination that brought them and all their children to America for good. Sojourners no longer. This is the story as my mother often told it. Only near the end of her life, did she fill in the part that brought back old hurt, the thing that happened one day while Miriam was gone. The episode has a villain, an old gossip in the village who informed my mother—then eight or nine—that Miriam had found a new husband in America. "She is never coming back." For the rest of that long year, my mother waited to see what would happen.

The passages below are from my book *Bint Arab: Arab and Arab American Women in the United States*. The first words of the title translate as "Arab girl" or "Arab daughter," but the phrase is also used, more generally, to refer to any female of Arab heritage. In telling its story of Arab-American women, *Bint Arab* draws on archival materials, the work of scholars, and, above all, on dozens of interviews. It also includes brief sections, like those that follow, in which I harvest memories of my mother. The final passage I've included here, cast as a letter that begins "Dear Mother," was written as the epilogue to the book.

When I wanted to go to college, my mother raised no objection, though neither was she convinced of the need for it. My father, it emerged, was harboring fantasies of a daughter at Bryn Mawr, for him the pinnacle of classiness. It wasn't just snob appeal. Compared to my mother, he had greater faith in the virtue of learning—all his aspirations took that turn, as did his vanity. When he died, he was still carrying in his pocket my third-grade report card with its unbroken ranks of straight A's and his five signatures (one for each term) in penmanship that curled like Arabic script.

I never applied to Bryn Mawr, and my father settled for his second choice, Wellesley. My mother was glad because it was only 20 minutes from home. She was growing old, she said, and waited for the implications to sink in. I lived on campus, anyway.

Though, like most Arabs, my mother, Hannah, loved poetry, aphorism, and elegant turns of phrase, she had little inclination toward learning in the abstract. Her deepest admiration was reserved for people who could do useful things—tailor a jacket, hang wallpaper, unjam a window, change a flat. She was handy herself. Standing watch over six looms had taught her the pirouettes of cogs and wheels and pulleys. And when one of her sewing machines acted up, she could often set it to rights with screwdriver, pliers, and bit of old curtain rod. At least she could try. It was as defeatist (and extravagant) to send for a repairman at the first sign of trouble as to call a doctor for every ache or fever.

Once, up on a chair to examine a light fixture, she fell and fractured her ankle, then hobbled around for 24 hours before letting me drive her to the doctor's office. Aspirin, she thought, could cure anything. And, in her case, she was nearly right. At 90, she took one pink pill a day for borderline hypertension, and that was it, except for a single Bayer on days when she felt "blue."

When she felt the lump in her breast, she kept it a secret, like her childhood terror that Miriam would never return, tracking its growth to the size of a fist. She must have told herself that nothing could be very wrong since she was not in pain and she was being a good girl now, seeing her doctor every three months. Humoring him. He'd take her blood pressure, listen to her heart, but never bothered to schedule a mammogram. "At her age, she'll never get breast cancer," he explained, "and even if she does, it won't grow." Sixteen lymph nodes tested positive.

There were things Hannah could never understand: how to read a map, why I wanted my own apartment, that a poem doesn't have to rhyme, that cancer doesn't have to hurt. But she read the *Christian Science Monitor* every day, and could tell you what was happening in remote parts of the world. She watched the Sunday morning talk shows too, though she was skeptical of the media in the way Arab-Americans often are. Her politics were mostly liberal, influenced probably by Wadie who, in the last decade of his life, supported Red China's bid for a UN seat and thought Truman was right to fire MacArthur. In religion, Hannah followed a middle road, not counting on eternity but never starting a journey or ending a day without asking God's blessing. In the morning, she was full of projects and plans she had cooked up during the night, not just for herself but for everyone she cared about. She could not let well enough alone.

I wanted peace; she wanted action, and she wanted it now. It set her teeth on edge to find me deep in a novel on a Saturday morning, the very time she and God had set aside for decent people to clean house. When I finally bestirred myself to help, I was still a sorry spectacle. Hannah would almost rather see me back in bed than plopped down on a dining-room chair, twisting myself every which way to dust it.

Years later, when I was Ph.D. student in literature, she'd see me with a book and ask what I was reading. "Stories," I'd tell her. "It's for school," I'd add, cutting the ground out from under her. It sounded crazy, but she couldn't be sure, and so I had her at a disadvantage. Until the summer day she caught me on the front porch with Chaucer. "What are you reading?" "Stories. Would you like to hear them?" And out spilled my giggly versions of the Miller's and the Reeve's tales. Now she was truly shocked and no mistake. Not so much by the arse-kissing and the pissing—her own sense of humor was too earthy for that—but that this was the stuff of my higher education. When she considered too the stories I told her about my classmates and professors, their affairs, divorces, and drug dealing, her disappointment was complete. "We used to respect educated people," she told me. "Oh, we thought they were high above us. But now my eyes are open. Your schooling has taught me a good lesson."

※

My first admirer was Robert Hope, the class showoff who swallowed ants, flies, and anything else the other kids fed him and whose lips were always blue from sucking on inky scraps of composition paper. He'd yank my thick pigtails when I wasn't looking and chase me home from school each day, careful never to catch me because what would he do with me then? Once, though, in a fit of malice, he got close enough to swipe at my arm and made me spill a stack of Christmas cards our teacher, Mr. Karp, had given me to mail. Envelopes upside down in the snow, white on white, I couldn't be sure I'd retrieved them all. Mr. Karp would be very angry, and he would blame me. When I tried to tell him about it the next day, I was so nervous I couldn't think of the word "I." "Me dropped your letters," I said.

When I reached the fifth grade, Ernest Donaruma, who lived in a fancy brick house on the West Roxbury Parkway, said would I go to the movies with him, then pinned me against a lamp post outside the schoolyard and pushed his face in close to kiss me. When I hollered and scratched him, he backed off in a hurry. After that, I wasn't sure the invitation was still open, but I liked Ernest, so I thought I'd just mention it to my mother. She kept saying, "What! What!" and that my father better not hear about this.

She hadn't taken that well, I thought. So I never told her about Edward Dunn, the new boy in class that my best friend Ruth and I tailed home one day, not knowing what else to do when we liked a boy. Ruth's parents were sober-faced Methodists, her father superintendent of the Sunday School; mine were Arabs who sent me out of the room whenever adult conversation threatened to take an interesting turn. Prissy and smug, Ruth and I made the mistake of hanging out with each other, instead of with the C+ run of girls, who were busily piecing together the facts of life.

When I finally got wind of how things were, I wanted to be sure. And I was mad. Why should everyone know but me? I found my mother upstairs in my bedroom, putting new white sheets on my bed. "I want you to tell me where babies come from," I screamed. And I made her do it. In two clipped sentences, which was all she could manage, she diagrammed the mechanics of sex. So it was true. It was awful. "You just have to put up with it," she said smoothing out the last wrinkle, "it doesn't take long."

And yet when I got my first period, she was all smiles, only astonished that I didn't know what was happening to me. Hadn't I heard girls talk? And no dire warning about boys. No curfews ever, or rules about where I could go or friends I could go with. (What awful thing does it say about me that she trusted me so?) No dates either, of course. I didn't much care except maybe when I missed my senior prom. But, since I went to an all-girls school, I would have had to do the asking, and though I fantasized all the time about boys, there was no flesh and blood specimen I could think of to be seen with. So my high school years passed without our ever having it out.

Once I got away to college, my parents couldn't stop me from dating—the little bit that I did date. They just looked the other way and trusted that, once I put my mind to it, I would meet some honorable young man from a good Arab family and marry him. But no hurry about that.

Meanwhile, there was Steve, the handsome WASP I dated for most of my junior year. ("How did you land *him*?" asked a friend I never forgave.) Once when I was home for the weekend, he picked me up and drove me back to campus. And then, a couple of times, he dropped by the house when I wasn't there, thinking he could charm my parents into liking him. They were always polite, would not have known how to be otherwise. But they must have wondered: who was this blond outlander and what did he want from them? Surely, not their daughter.

That spring break, Steve came by the house again, and we went out somewhere—a party, a movie, bowling, I don't remember. Then came back late, parked the old VW bug down the street, and made out for an hour. At one point, the neighborhood cop, walking his beat, stopped to peer into the car, but when he saw it was only me, he smiled and moved on. My mother met me at the door, beside herself with fury and, I suppose, with panic. Where had I been? Wretch that I was, what had I been doing? She would not let me go to bed until I told. There was so little to tell, but even that little would have been too much for her. It had been a late party—or movie, or string— I said. What was the problem?

She scared me that night. I'd been pretending to myself that I could go and come as I pleased; I'd forgotten what she could never forget, the village culture in her bones, the dread of being shamed, never able to marry off your children or visit your neighbor, the misery of having everyone look through you as if you had ceased to exist or were less than the dirt under their feet. Born in the 19th century and into another world, old enough to be my grandmother, she did her best. And I learned to do my part, lying and leading a double life, anything rather than rouse again that killing rage.

※

Hannah was a charter member of the Ladies' Aid and for many years, because her Arabic was good, its recording secretary. As long as she was single—that is, for 15 years into the life of the club—custom prevented her from moving up to the presidency. But the moment she married, she was elected to that office, as if it had been reserved for her all along.

By then, admirable stage presence and a voice that carried without a microphone had made Hannah the club's chief orator. In later years, she loved to tell about the evening she spoke, as always in Arabic, at the burning of the club's mortgage, while seated behind her on stage was James Michael Curley ("Vote early! Vote often!"), the rascal mayor of Boston. As she turned from the podium, Curley—that master of ethnic politics—took her hand, congratulated her on her speech, told her he'd understood every word. "Wasn't he silly!" she'd laugh happily, recalling that bright moment, and it would bother me every time that he had charmed her so easily.

The last time Hannah took the stage was at the club's 70th anniversary celebration, when she was 92. She recited from memory a long, light-hearted poem on uppity clubwomen that her brother Litfallah had written half a century earlier in immigrant-speak, a comic mix of colloquial Arabic and broken English. Midway through the 200 lines or so, her shoulders and arms and hands began to tremble, but her voice was strong to the end, and her recall perfect.

Hannah's five brothers were long dead by then, and the glory days of the club long over. But years before, Naseeb had carefully labeled and stored away a record of those days—over 30 years of club minutes, most of them in Hannah's own hand. For many months, she and I had been reviewing them—usually after supper on as many evenings as I could manage. She read, translated, reminisced; I asked questions and took notes. It wasn't always harmonious—sometimes I'd prod and push for answers she didn't have; she'd get fed up or tired and threaten to quit. But mostly it was companionable. For once, our enthusiasms had come together—I wanting to know about the past, she wanting to relive it, both of us determined to see the task through to its end. Two days after her mastectomy, Hannah was propped up in a hospital bed, minutes again in hand, concentrating, and I—feet resting on the foot of her bed—was still taking notes. It was not a bad way to heal.

�֍

Dear Mother,

Strange that I associate the word "pious" with you. You were not pious in any conventional sense, never hanging gilded icons above your bed or caring two cents about church doctrine. You judged each new priest—most *im*piously I used to think—primarily by how well he sang the service. (You liked a good performance when you looked in each year.) Otherwise, if he kept his opinions to himself, you had no quarrel with him. And if he looked forward to coffee in your kitchen, after sprinkling upstairs and down with holy water, and could tell a good story, you declared him as fine a priest as one could reasonably expect.

Pious in what way, then? Perhaps in respecting all variety of creature (flies buzzing round your dishpan lived to buzz another day) and believing, for all your humor, that some few things were to be taken seriously. Not just the looking out for family (that was nature, no special merit there) but the claims of neighbor and community. "What does she do for others?" you complained on cue, whenever the conversation turned to a particular in-law who spent her days tending her own grapevine. You never understood, I think, that some people need all their strength just to get *themselves* through the day.

And for sure, you were patting yourself on the back—remembering your years of service to the Ladies' Aid—but I never begrudged you that vanity. You tried to make a place for me too in the club, enrolling me at birth, paying my dues punctually year after year. Grown up, I would sometimes act the member—attend a meeting, write a press release, model hats at a fund raiser. But it was all play. I didn't have the calling.

I wonder now how seriously you would take this book, over which your spirit presides. You'd be pleased, at least, at the company I've been keeping. It irritated you that the girlfriends I brought home (and that you charmed) were Irish, German, Norwegian, or, most often, Jewish (though Jews, you said, were practically our cousins).

You would have settled for just one *bint arab*. Now here's a bookful for you. Or a houseful, all branches of the family converging. Doors thrown open to old and young and middle-aged, Muslim and Christian, Algerian and Palestinian, Iraqi and Egyptian, Syrian and Lebanese, all the kin. "*Ahlan wa sahlan*, my home is yours. My book is yours!"

As long as I'm showing to such good advantage, I might just hint that doing for others can take many forms, including this text, which (in imagination) I push over to your side of the table. "Yes," you say, paging through it with curiosity. But I see you have reservations. You know me as one knows an old antagonist and are used to looking for the corner left undusted. It will not long escape your eye, the absence of a final setting to rights, a housewifely conclusion that clears the dishes, sweeps the crumbs, hangs up the apron, and slips each guest a bag of goodies to be carried home.

Look, here's the best I can do. (Let's settle for a lived-in look.) This house, this text, is full of voices tumbling over one another. Point and counterpoint, yes and no. Issues worried in every room, on every story (*in* every story) from generation to generation: how to be a good daughter, sister, wife, mother, how to be a good Arab, how (pay good heed) to survive. In the house our mothers built—yes your mother too—shame lurked at every landing, so we proceeded cautiously, ears cocked to hear others (*nnaas*) whispering. Hearts divided between two urges. The need to make a getaway (crash out the back door, run for your life), the need to belong (pull up to the table with women who call you "sister" and know your people for three generations back). Mother, you remember. Clutter of right and wrong and second thoughts, curtains of laughter, candles of affection. And finally, after half a lifetime staring out the window, planting in the garden, smiling at the neighbors, passage into a new identity, neither *Arab* nor *Ameerkan*.

A new story to tell the children.

In the first years of the twentieth century, Arabs, like many other immigrants of that time, hired on as mill hands and factory workers. But a number also went into business for themselves, usually as peddlers or small merchants or, like my mother, garment makers. A handful struck out down a more exotic path, finding their niches in the fringe world of circuses and fairs. The best known of their number was George Hamid, who learned to tumble on the streets of his hometown in Lebanon, then became part of an acrobatic group that toured with Buffalo Bill's Wild West show; Annie Oakley, also with the show, gave him his first lessons in reading and writing English. Eventually, Hamid became an Atlantic City impresario and cofounder of the circus that still bears his name. Though not nearly so successful, my mother's brother Naseeb made a decent living in the "amusement" business. This, after my mother had tried to coax him into an honest trade like barbering. The roller coaster Naseeb and his partner owned (together with Dodgems, a shooting gallery, a Tunnel of Love—the list goes on) was the towering centerpiece of Revere Beach, just across the water from Boston's Logan Airport. The very same beach to which the writer Mary Antin's Jewish family had moved upon their arrival from Russia many decades earlier.

In her classic 1912 autobiography, *The Promised Land*, Antin remembered the beach of her childhood as pristine. "No boulevards," she wrote, "no stately bath-houses, no hotels, no gaudy amusement places, no illuminations, no showmen, no tawdry rabble." Intrusions that were entrenched by the time she took pen in hand. And that I remember from my own childhood, years later. I am, I suppose, as nostalgic for the teeming crowds (I would not call them "tawdry rabble") and the neon lights as Antin was for that earlier "bright clean sweep of sand." But, even in the idyll that Antin recreated in her memoir, commercialism had made inroads. Her own father ran a beach stand that sold ice cream, lemonade and sausages, hot peanuts and pink popcorn, to city people arriving by train to spend a day by the sea.

To many Americans (and, no doubt, to Antin), a living that fed off amusement parks might have seemed disreputable. But not to me. On the contrary, I saw my uncle's line of work as the badge of his respectability. It was an open-air, all-American enterprise he ran, far removed from the lint-ridden factories and hole-in-the-wall groceries that other family and friends were consigned to for long hours each day. For sure, it brought in more dollars than their jobs did, enough so that he could buy a red-brick colonial in an upscale suburban neighborhood. And, between Labor Day and Memorial Day, could sleep late, go to his "club" (a storefront where Arab-American men played backgammon or cards for money—the cop on the beat was paid to look the other way) or have his buddies over in the evening for whiskey, Cuban cigars, and more rounds of poker or gin rummy. My aunt fretted. Not good for a man to have so much time on his hands, she said. But, like a good wife, she brought the men coffee and a mess of *mezza*—sliced cucumbers, salted chickpeas, pistachios in the shell, olives, cheeses, and Syrian bread—and emptied ashtrays.

But in my eyes, it wasn't just the roller coaster or the nice house that made my uncle and his family more "American" than my own and more solidly middle class. It was the accumulated detail of their lives: the baby grand on which my cousins took music lessons; the Baptist Church they attended and the minister they had to Sunday dinner; the fact that my uncle belonged to the Rotary Club and the Masons and voted Republican; the fact that my aunt was—in today's parlance—a stay-at-home mom. When my cousins came through the door after school she was there to whip up a snack, and, if they'd brought friends along, so much the better.

My uncle and aunt certainly never shunned the Arab community. (Though their children, I think, were just as glad to.) They were deeply invested in its members and its institutions; within it, they found their deepest attachments. But, more than my parents, each had both the desire and the know-how to socialize with outsiders. My uncle's business interests encouraged intercourse with men of other ethnic persuasions; so too did the fraternal order to which he belonged. As for my aunt, the American mission school she attended as a child in Lebanon had fostered the knack of moving with some ease between two worlds.

Still, in the end, it was the glitzy roller coaster that gave me bragging rights among my friends and helped situate me closer to the American norm that was always just beyond my reach.

Evelyn with family in front of the Cyclone roller coaster

Revere Beach

THE RETURN

Once a year, if that, I drive the old familiar route. Wind along the Jamaicaway and on to Storrow Drive, keeping the Charles on my left, the backside of Beacon Hill on my right as I run the rim of the city before shooting north through the tunnel or over the bridge. If I choose the bridge, as I usually do, I watch for the masts of Old Ironsides rocking below, old bones in a cradle. And on the opposite shore, Bunker Hill Monument, an obelisk keeping its distance from a rabble of smokestacks. The neighborhood is not what it used to be.

Ten minutes and the first whiff of salt air. When the sea glints ahead, I am relieved. The reassurance one feels finding someone at home to answer one's knock on the door. Pretending that inside things are the same though the old furnishings were carted long ago to the dump or given away.

The waves still roll in, but the Revere Beach of my childhood is gone. It's been 25 years since rides and concessions last elbowed each other on the boulevard fronting the sea—penny arcade (slot machines spitting out weight, fortune, photos of Rita Hayworth, David Niven,

Evelyn Shakir

Bing Crosby), Dodgems ("no head-on collisions" but we did), rat-a-tat shooting galleries with cookie-cutter ducks on parade and tiers of kewpie-doll prizes. Food stands in action—franks on the grill, clams in a Fryolator, peppersteak sizzling, corn popping frantic in a display case, sugar and food dye spinning pink cotton candy, frozen custard (banana my favorite) spiraling thick-tongued into waffle cones, then dipped headfirst in jimmies. We circled too—Ferris wheels (single and double) and musical merry-go-rounds (took us years to figure out the outside horses went fastest); Whip, Tilt-a-Whirl, Bubble Bounce; the Loop-the-Loop flipping us head over heels; skeletons dangling in the Tunnel of Love. Bluebeard's Castle: shifting walkways, mirrors stretching us skinny or squat, jets of air hiking our skirts. Us shrieking.

Above all, the Cyclone, my uncle's roller coaster, the brawniest ride on the beach. Five hundred feet long, more than 100 feet high, its trains clocked at 50 miles an hour (faster, we bragged, than the coaster at Coney Island), the Cyclone dominated the boulevard and the horizon. By day a rational geometry of ellipses and parabolas; at night a turreted castle lighting the sky. The old hands on the Cyclone called my uncle "the chief" and so did my aunt. But to me he was king; his wife, consort; his kids next-in-line; and, by right of blood, I was royalty too. Summer days I strolled the boulevard in bathing suit and sandals and shorts like anyone else's, hugging my secret identity.

But when it was time for lunch or I needed a bathroom, I turned back to the coaster and whipped under a turnstile, like Clark Kent into a phone booth. Then ran up the down ramp, dodging patrons ("Hey, kid, where you going?" as if I owed them a password), and raced the length of the platform, tracks below to my left, my uncle's office door on the far side, above it the sign, "Safest Ride on the Beach." Next I slowed for the narrows ahead. There, a wall jutting out from the right allowed space for only one person to pass, and that cautiously. The royal guard, I thought, if there were a royal guard,

32

could pick off attackers. One by one, enemy soldiers would topple onto the rails, wounded and whimpering. And even if I wanted to help, they'd be too heavy, and I'd be too late. No time before the next car bore down the track, mangling them horribly.

When the platform widened again and I could breathe, I'd pick up speed, veering right and then left into the cottage where my uncle's family stayed all summer, tucked in the foothills of the roller coaster.

THE ROOF

Or, after turning right, I could keep going straight and up three stairs onto the roof of the souvenir shop below. With planking laid over, it was front porch and playground. ("Don't run," warned my aunt. "Don't get too close to the edge.") During the day, a private place for my older cousin Sally and me to lay down towels and tan until the sting of the sun drove us inside and we discovered, always too late, that our backs were strawberry red and we'd be sleeping that night on our tummies.

Another picture stays with me. It's sunset. My aunt stands on the roof, hand shading her eyes. I follow her gaze to the peak of the Cyclone and the American flag carrying on in the wind. At the foot of the flagpole, her son. I know what he's done. Hitched a ride to the top and stepped out. Had enough time—gauged it right—to swing clear before the train he'd been riding lunged down the slope. I've seen him do it before, him or one of the men. Each day at this hour, someone rides up there to haul down the flag and carry it back down the hill. On the platform again, Eddie glances our way in time to see his mother hurry inside, her thoughts already on supper, her own performance soon on the line.

After supper, with the cottage still holding the heat of the day, the roof summoned everyone—friends, family, cousins visiting from the old country. Men first, then children, then women, we ascended to the ocean breeze against our skin, grownups balancing cups of Turkish coffee in one hand, and, if they were needed, hoisting kitchen chairs with the other. Smokes bulged in shirt pockets and apron pockets: cigars, Lucky Strikes, Philip Morris.

Now, at the end of the day, it was our parents' turn to chat, the children's turn to listen or not as we pleased. Rivalries, recipes, surgery, shoe sales—subjects swirled up, then subsided. The weather, the church, the A-bomb, the olive trees of Mount Lebanon. Conversation rummaged like wind across sand, picking up this scrap or that, tumbling it, teasing out meaning, before dropping it yards further along. Until finally, my aunt or someone would remember to ask, "Who wants frozen custard?" Then she and my mother competed to stuff dollar bills in our hands, insisting (no matter what anyone said) "Bring back for everyone," and we'd count heads.

All evening, seated in Adirondack chairs or kitchen chairs or on a bench, we looked across at the darkening sea that blossomed white on the shore, and down at the crowd that circulated, loose-limbed, along the boulevard. In and out of our frame, people passed, and we'd follow with lazy eyes two teenagers holding hands, a grandmother in earrings and nylons licking ice cream into a peak, an ex-sailor with a navy blanket rolled under one arm and a toddler sailing smartly along on his shoulders. We saw colored people up close, strolling and eating and laughing as if they were white, and we wondered what went on in their heads. "Do you think they love their children like we do?" asked my mother. No one could say. When a constellation of people caught my particular fancy, I'd keep them in sight, craning my neck to follow until they melted into the crowd and the night, and then I'd look out for their return. As glad to see them again as if they were friends come back to bid a proper good-night.

Or actors back for a final bow. Because the street was our theater, our stage. We peered down from our balcony and saw the performers as clearly as God sees his creatures. They were caught unawares, unconscious of critics at work, passing judgment on their dress, their weight, the family dramas we built out of a woman's scowl or a man's arm circling her waist. Every time the Cyclone plummeted behind us and riders screamed, the action would shift, a few heads look up. But as if fairy dust had been thrown in their eyes, the people below never saw us. Night or day, it was the same. We looked down on them with impunity.

If they had seen us, those people gazing over our heads, if they'd once dropped their gaze 10 degrees, they'd have caught us in our own pantomime. Puppet faces peeking over the scalloped parapet rimmed with lights that ran the length of the Cyclone. They'd have spied, like a painted backdrop, the roof and chimney of a fanciful cottage set in a woodland of white scaffolding. Seen my aunt's laundry—dish towels, flowered aprons, white sheets and underwear—verisimilitude billowing on the clothesline.

THE COASTER

Inside the cottage, we lived all day in the shadow of the roller coaster, sensitive to its moods. In the morning it slept, oblivious, while through the kitchen window we glimpsed Whitey, the caretaker, toolbox in hand, walking the track as he did every day, spitting tobacco, tightening bolts. After lunch we listened for the test run that came at one on the dot. Frisky, on edge, the train took that first daring plunge and then, for sheer joy of the dance, shot up into space and whipped back like a boomerang. Like the flash of a scythe.

All afternoon and into the night, the train made its rounds, dipping and climbing, pouncing from hillside to valley, from high notes to low in predictable sequence, flattening finally into a coda. Then, after a pause, starting up again as if someone had cried, "From the top!" So much commotion outside, while inside, busy in the forefront of our lives, we pursued our humdrum ways. My aunt stuffed grape leaves for supper, Sally practiced a tango, the boys tuned in to the Red Sox, and, at two, my uncle came in for his afternoon nap on the sofa. That was the signal to hush the children and hurry us out the door. Big kids and little gathered blankets and towels and shovels and pails and headed again to the beach. Hours later, we came back salty and brown as fried clams, brushing sand off our feet and calling for whoever was up to unhook the screen door.

As long as the Cyclone kept to its beat, we kept to ours. Looked up, uneasy, only when quiet sounded for minutes on end. Was business bad? Had something gone wrong? My aunt, though a Baptist, made the sign of the cross. When all was right with the world, we lived suspended between sea and mountain. The roar of the coaster overhead was our waterfall, the shrieks of the riders our bird calls. Each hill, each habitat heard from, each cry with distinct pitch and meaning.

At the end of the run, as the train rounded the bend and barreled home down the straight, the cottage took notice at last. Walls, windows, and studs, shivering helplessly.

THE BATHROOM

The house must have been built in two stages, space added on as the family grew. Because in the very center was the bathroom that smelled of Ivory soap and Lysol and was circled by six other rooms. It had two doors on facing walls, one into Sally's bedroom, the other into the room with the extra bed. But even if you remembered to lock both doors (and later unlock them), you couldn't relax. Because on a third wall, by the commode, was a window with sashes and curtains and shade, which must once have looked out on the Cyclone, its homestretch of track. But now it looked only into the bedroom shared by Eddie and Jimmie, and nothing delighted them more than threatening to peek. So no matter how much I needed to pee, I first had to lower the window and lock it, and then pull down the shade all the way. Even then, I could hear those bad boys calling my name on the other side of the pane. Until, to save my life, I couldn't do my business.

In every other room of the house, Eddie and Jimmie ignored me. Sally, who found me occasionally useful, let me brush her black hair, which fell straight to her shoulders. While I was pinning it into an updo, she'd entertain questions about nail buffers, ballet slippers, and Pond's enriched night cream. A few days of that and she'd begin sighing a lot, and in each sigh I'd hear her wanting her room to herself again. Wishing me home. But she was ugly mean only when her particular girlfriend came over and started tormenting me.

"I saw you on the beach," the girl mocked. "You were flirting with the boys and shaking your little behind!"

"No, I wasn't, don't you say that!" Her fibbing worked me up into a miserable state.

And then Sally forgot she was a big teenager and I was her little cousin. "I saw you too," she sang out, "and I'm gonna tell."

Her mother, she meant. But in that house, grownup ladies were usually not a source of danger. My aunt gave me good things to eat, called me her dear, and didn't ever get mad. My mother, happy to be with her brother and off work for a week, forgot to point out the things I did wrong every day. But sometimes they scared me—my mother, my aunt, and her cousins Lillian and Rose. It was when they were getting ready to go across to the beach. I'd watch them coming, in turn, out of the bathroom. Their black bathing suits not yet pulled up all the way, their oversized helpings of breast hanging out, secrets they usually hid inside their dresses or under their bathrobes. And always, as they pulled up their straps in front of the mirror and reached in to arrange handfuls of flesh, they were laughing together, louder than I could ever remember. And I didn't know why and I couldn't guess who they were any more.

On an everyday basis, it was my uncle who worried me most. Who, everyone said, was such a good man. Even though he drank, smoked, wagered at cards, and had a revolver for when he took the Cyclone receipts to the bank late at night. Once, he forgot to lock it away. The next day, when my aunt saw the bulge in the jacket he'd hung by the door, she was beside herself. "The children, the children!" That day I learned that I must never touch that gun, not even by accident, because it would explode in my hand and someone would die, just as I must never touch the red switch in Sally's bedroom that would bring policemen running. (I dreamed jail cells and electric chairs.) So many dangers to remember, and—except for the gypsy in the dirty scarf who told fortunes on the beach and whom my aunt befriended—all of them to do with my uncle. But those people who said my aunt was lucky, I think I know now what they meant. That he was a good provider and generous to family and friends, that (unlike my father) he was usually even-tempered, and that he kept his own counsel, as a man should do.

Except once at dinner, pouring himself a third jigger of whiskey, he looked up at me. "You're a spoiled brat." My face got hot and my eyes swam with tears (though I wasn't a little girl any more), and the table got quiet. My aunt, I think, cried out a quick reproach. But in the instant he spoke, I knew my uncle had been itching to call me that name, had been saying it behind my back for who knew how many days and waiting to corner me, without my mother around. And while he waited, his snow-cold anger building on itself had drifted higher and higher. And I, seated at his table that day, a fork halfway to my mouth, hadn't even noticed it was winter.

But I was afraid of him long before that, and, when I try to think why, I have to scrounge for reasons. Maybe because he got up late in the morning (not like my father who took the bus and the El and spent all day hunched over a printing press). Maybe because he was out of the house late at night (not like my father who read and paced the living room and groaned before going to bed at 10). Maybe because he had a gun or because he had a hearing aid, with a battery big as a pack of cigars, that filled his shirt pocket. Or maybe because he was king and everyone had to give way to him. I remember a rule. "Don't go in the bathroom when your uncle needs to use it."

What did that mean? How could I know? When I woke up in the morning, I'd lie still on the couch in Sally's room and wonder and wonder if I should risk a quick pee. And always, it seemed, before I could make up my mind to act, I'd hear my uncle chugging awake, coughing, choking until I thought his lungs would tear open and he would die if I foolishly got up and got in his way.

As it happened, he did die of lung trouble, and so later did Eddie and, before him, Sally, who despised cigarettes and had never smoked in her life. Jimmy just moved away. My aunt lived on by herself, her goal to die in her own house as my mother had done. But it didn't work out. "There's something wrong with me," she confided when I dropped by one afternoon, bringing her my company, better than none, a thank-you for those early days. "Up here," she explained, her fingers fluttering at her temples. And she was right. The last two years of her life were spent in a nursing home, where she forgot that her parents and husband and two of her children were dead, and then forgot them entirely and the Cyclone and everything else.

THE FOURTH OF JULY

On the Fourth, new satellites appeared in our orbit, second cousins and such I wouldn't see again for a year. My aunt sent out for hot dogs and clam rolls and root beer, though mostly the visitors stuck to the beach, swimming and sunning and hitting the food stalls themselves. In the evening, those still on hand came into the house to share in the big night ahead.

Outside, after the suppertime lull, the night crowd would start pulling in, and soon, by the thousands, they'd be swarming off of the pavement and into the street and the good times would roll. If the weather held, the Cyclone would run three trains at a time; just two, and the summer (everyone said) was a failure. From the roof, we counted the crowd lined up on the platform, willed it to multiply. Like playing with fire. "Safest ride on the beach," but collision kept crossing our minds.

That night it took five experienced workers to man the platform, one at the first brake, one at the second, and three to punch tickets. "Ride again," they coaxed. "Ride again, 20 cents!" The operation ran like a musical round, one train leaving the platform as another pulled in, while a third careened in mid-flight. High-pressure work it was, unloading and reloading the cars with only seconds to spare; every hour or two, one man on the platform spelling another, and sometimes my uncle himself working a shift. After midnight, my aunt sent out trays piled high with egg salad and ham-and-cheese sandwiches and pots of hot coffee.

The climax, toward which everything tended, was the display of fireworks—advertised, of course, for a particular hour, but those who had the say allowed themselves plenty of slack. If the go-ahead came too soon, the crowds would dissipate early, unspent dollars carried home in their pockets or purses. But delay too long, and people got tired and angry. Next year they might take the boat to Nantasket or find someone with room in his car who was off to the Cape for the day.

Just when we couldn't wait any more, we'd hear the first firing and converge on the roof to chorus our ritual oohs and aahs as giant red chrysanthemums ballooned overhead before burning out, one star at a time; as peonies broke, first blue, then red, then gold until their breath gave out; as weeping willows cascaded into the sea, orange embers trailing white smoke. On the roof, everyone had an opinion, balancing this year's spectacle against last year's—pleased if my uncle, who'd footed a chunk of the bill, had gotten his money's worth, indignant if he hadn't. After 30 minutes, the finale: a deafening fuselage of rockets turning the sky milky white, a single farewell salute, and then silence except for yelps and whines from Fritz the Spitz, poor creature, still in the house. Leashed to a doorknob, left to cope on his own.

With the Cyclone still going strong but the children in bed, grownups sat up sometimes till dawn. As I drifted into sleep, I could hear them chatting and laughing and shushing each other. Creating, for once, a world that felt perfectly safe.

Early the next morning, my aunt played pied piper. Herding the children into the sitting room and down a dark staircase. Then through a door, and into the fenced-in yard where the Cyclone braced its forest of timbers, and the sun came through only in patches. A secret landscape of hulking, lumbering shapes. And (secret within a secret) a wooden garage where my uncle parked his Oldsmobile. Opposite the garage, a wide gate in the fence let out on the back street, taking pedestrians by surprise. They'd stare as the silver Olds made its exit, my uncle's eyes masked by sunglasses. "Who was that man?" bystanders asked. Or so I liked to imagine.

The staircase down, the garage: other days they made me think of Batman and Robin dropping into the Batmobile and speeding away to fight evil. Except that my uncle was partnered with only my aunt and probably just out after groceries.

The wilderness under the roller coaster was nowhere for a child on her own, but I stuck close to my aunt. She'd troop us down the morning of the Fifth to scavenge for treasure, coins and bills that had jumped from men's pockets the night before as the coaster swooshed overhead. Other stuff, too, on the ground—keys, kerchiefs, cracked eyeglasses, hair combs galore, an occasional camera. Once Whitey found dentures and another time a toupee. Items not smashed and of value we turned in at the office. But the cash was ours to keep and to count all through breakfast.

The Fourth at Revere was a ritual my mother insisted upon and that I never thought to question. It was years before I heard the story of Mr. C, a friend of the family, who had owned another coaster on the beach. One Fourth, he rode up on the Thunderbolt, in order to check out a stretch of rail. When the train came down again, his seat was empty. Searchers found the body below a 70-foot dip. That holiday my mother had broken her pattern, stayed at home or maybe gone to her in-laws. Never again, she decided. And as long as my uncle lived, she was there on the Fourth of July, keeping her promise.

THE OWNER

Another thing it took me years to discover was that my uncle did not own the Cyclone outright. In fact, he held only 49 percent of the stock in the corporation, his partner the other 51. In case of dispute, my uncle could never prevail. And yet, as far as I could see, the partner put in only brief appearances on the premises, coming in once a day to nap on a cot and pick up his mail. While my uncle gamely took care, keeping the books, supervising the men, seeing that the Cyclone was properly groomed. Living in its bowels 24 hours a day. The roller coaster meant more to him than to anyone, a brimming 100 percent.

REMAINS

The brick bathhouse remains, that rented swimsuits. The Italianate-style police station also, as well as the bandstand and the pavilion in which the deaf and dumb (what people still called them) convened and signed the day away. The crescent beach itself endures, of course, and the gulls. And people still sit on stonewalls looking out at the sea. They still swim, still loll on the sand and stroll the boulevard.

But their numbers are far fewer, and most live so much in the present, too young to remember the way things were, not used to wondering. Apartment buildings rise next to where the Cyclone did, but even taller. One fish place still does a box-office business, its customers locals or people who have driven the few miles from East Boston and Charlestown or sometimes, like me, from the leafier suburbs. It's those cars that tell the story. As soon as masses of people could afford them, Revere lost its reason for being.

In its day, it had catered to blue-collar laborers and white-collar clerks and anyone else who depended on public transportation. For 10 cents, the MTA shuttled them in from every neighborhood of the city—Yankees and immigrant families, colored people, and servicemen on leave. Come to enjoy the beach and the special attractions—beauty pageants, dance marathons, parachute jumpers, Miss Victory shot from a cannon, a horse with a girl on its back diving 40 feet into a water tank. Through the 1930s and 40s, crowds of over 100,000, sometimes 200,000, showed up on a summer Saturday or Sunday. Strangers, yes, but at least riding the same waves, catching the same rays, holding on for dear life on the same horseshoe curve of the roller coaster. A gift.

Until affluence made that gift superfluous.

By the mid-seventies, it was over. The stands torn down, the Cyclone razed, its yard grassed over. What had been, relegated to souvenir posters and T-shirts, recalled in anniversary issues of the local paper. Recently, I met a woman from California who had grown up, she told me, in East Boston. "Remember Revere Beach?" she asked me. "Remember the roller coaster—oh, what was it called?" And then without prompting she came up with it. "The Cyclone!" she trumpeted, pleased as people my age always are when they can conjure up a name.

"My uncle owned the Cyclone," I couldn't wait to tell her.

"Six degrees of separation," her husband murmured.

"Oh, much less," she said, looking at me as if she'd stumbled on a distant cousin or an exiled aristocrat.

THE SEA

The sea is the sea is the sea. Exactly as you imagine and long for it if you have once awakened to the dazzle of sunlight on waves, or felt the flexing, insistent tide pull you down into sleep. At Revere, we played in the surf for hours, paddling close to shore, dancing Ring-Around-the-Rosy, teasing each other with seaweed "No, not tired," we insisted. "No, we haven't had enough!" I, who was frightened by everything, was never scared of the ocean. Though for days I picked my way along the bottom with care after seeing a beautiful boy, his foot slashed and bleeding, carried off by his friends. Then I grew reckless again. Only decades later, on an unfamiliar beach, did I come close to paying the price. A gray day, nothing violent, just the floor falling away under my feet. From the shore, strangers swam out to tow me in, almost not making it. How do you say "thank you" when teenage girls hand you your life before going back to their Cokes and their towels? High-schoolers in perky bikinis, toenails painted green.

I think of them now and remember the days when men could not bare their chests on the boulevard for fear of being cited and fined. When women wore black wool swimsuits and white rubber caps with straps under the chin, and white rubber slippers just to be safe. Against sharp rocks, broken shells, and anything else untoward that lurks under the waves.

Some 25 years had passed since my first trip to Lebanon. In the interim, the country had been savaged by civil war, foreign invasion, and the deliberate slaughter of civilians. Americans had been targeted: in 1983, an attack on the American embassy by a suicide bomber killed dozens of staff members; six months later, a similar attack on an American barracks took the lives of hundreds of Marines. Such traumas root deep; 15 years later, the State Department was still warning Americans to stay away or, at the least, to proceed with caution. At that moment, a friend suggested that I apply for a Fulbright grant that would subsidize my teaching for a term somewhere in the Arab world. I quickly warmed to the idea, but Lebanon, as I soon discovered, was out of the question; the Fulbright program there had shut down in the middle of the fighting and never yet reopened.

But living for a stretch in Palestine was also an exciting prospect, so I was pleased when the offer came of a position at the Islamic University in Gaza. If it was something different I was after, that would surely fill the bill. Even the knowledge that I would have to cover my hair and avoid the men's campus did not appreciably dampen my enthusiasm. What did trouble me was the university's expectation that I would carry a full teaching load. Impossible, I thought, since my Fulbright grant specified that half my time overseas be dedicated to doing research. I was still making my case to the Gazans when word came that all Fulbrights to Palestine had been withdrawn. It was now deemed too risky there for Americans.

One door closes, another opens. The e-mail read, "How would you like to go to Lebanon?" At the 11th hour, the State Department had had a change of heart. The bulletins it issued were catching up with the reality on the ground. I wonder too if someone thought to say, "Look folks, we have a Fulbright Fellow here of Lebanese heritage, vetted and approved, but no place to go. Why not let her test the waters?"

II
Teaching Abroad

Evelyn in Beirut

A Fulbright in Lebanon

BEIRUT

When neighbors and friends heard I'd soon be off to Beirut, they started treating me with new gentleness. As if I'd announced a terminal illness. "Take care of yourself," more than one said, patting my hand. Others said outright: "You're so brave!" Though it was *foolish*, they probably meant.

For someone like me who expects not just planes she's in, but even elevators, to crash without notice, this was heady stuff. Suddenly, I was Evelyn the Fearless. But, when you came down to it, I insisted, what was there really to fear? Americans weren't being kidnapped; the unspeakable civil war had been shut down for a decade; and I wouldn't be stupid enough to head south, toward the dangerous border with Israel.

Nothing I said made a difference. That last week, my friends hugged me as if they knew and I knew they might never see me again.

This was my second visit. I'd been to Lebanon in '72. In what people remember now as the golden age before the war. When snow-capped Lebanon was billed as the Switzerland of the Middle East, and Beirut was supposed to be Paris. That time I'd been part of a trend called "finding your roots." I'd visited my father's hometown and my mother's village, checked out Roman ruins and groves of ancient cedars, eaten grapes off the vine and dates off the tree and learned to drink arak. And—what I didn't write home about—flirted with cousins. Let them romance me.

Now, almost three decades later, I was traveling on more sober business. The first Fulbright fellow our government had sent to Lebanon—or so I was told—in over 15 years. There to teach university students and interview women.

I settled down in a small hotel in Hamra, the neighborhood of Beirut that stretches between the two American universities and is skirted by the sea. Just 50 years ago it was a suburban retreat with dirt roads, gardens, and the occasional stray sheep. Today it is urban with a vengeance. Paved over, congested, pulsating with life.

It is also one of the rare neighborhoods in Beirut where Muslims, Christians, and Druze are equally at home. In the early years of the civil war, residents took comfort in that circumstance. Thought no militia would want to chance hitting its own people. But there was no escaping this war. Leila pointed out the bullet holes in her balcony and told me about the militiamen who had taken over a floor in her building, just one flight down. And there was no escaping the Israeli invasion when it came. Christine remembered a time when bombardment—from the sky, from the sea, from the mountains—didn't let up for 30 hours. After 12, out of sheer obstinacy, she came up from the shelter, put on a red dress and went for a walk on the beach. There she met militiamen drunk or high on drugs. They offered her coffee.

Sometimes Hamra *was* a refuge, for people fleeing danger elsewhere. I stood with Mona at her window overlooking a small park. Each day she'd gauged how bad the fighting was outside the city by the number of squatters under the trees, families who came and went with prayer rugs, household utensils, and, once, a washing machine.

Such scenes were now comfortably in the past. Despite soldiers with machine guns guarding government buildings—or maybe because of them—the mean streets of Beirut, as far as I could tell, were perfectly benign. Even after dark I walked out alone—to the library, the grocery, the cyber café—and felt safer than I do at home.

But if I felt safe in Lebanon, American diplomats did not. The American embassy, rebuilt in the hills over Beirut, looks like—and is—a fortress. American personnel do not leave the compound without filing a written request and getting permission. Setting up appointments with people outside requires two phone calls—one to arrange the place, the other the time. To keep those engagements, Americans travel in bulletproof sedans, with driver and bodyguard, and follow rules about which seat to take and who opens the door. And, like teenagers with a curfew, they're expected home on the dot.

As a Fulbright, I was tethered, however loosely, to the embassy. On the other hand, I was a civilian. The staff weren't sure what rules should apply. Why worry them, I thought. I won't ask. Just go and come as I please, like a tourist.

And so one day I did what I'd told my friends back home I'd never do. I headed south, toward (but not into) the belt of Lebanese soil then still occupied by Israel. With me, a driver and a guide. Our destination the ruins of ancient Sidon, where Crusaders built a castle on the sea. And ancient Tyre, whose King Hiram sent lumber and workmen to build Solomon's great temple in Jerusalem.

The further south we drove, the more I realized this was a far cry from cosmopolitan Hamra. We were into Hizballah territory. Huge political posters hung everywhere: faces of Shia religious leaders and of young people, hailed as political martyrs—guerillas, I supposed, perhaps suicide bombers.

And then I saw a poster. The American flag, stripes running vertical, and dropping from each stripe, a bomb. On the field of blue, instead of 50 stars, 50 human skulls. At the bottom, in English, was written, "America, the cause of all our disasters."

A month after my return to Boston, seven Israeli soldiers in southern Lebanon were killed within the space of a few days. In the week that followed, Israeli planes flew dozens of sorties over Lebanon, knocking out power plants, killing civilians, reenacting something that might not have been war, but was nothing you and I would call peace. As I read the papers, listened to the BBC, and got through once on the phone, I worried about my new friends in Hamra. Imagined them hearing enemy planes roar overhead, feeling their way along blacked-out streets, choking on air thick with the smoke of private electrical generators. After midnight no power at all to be had. People shivering till dawn in unheated apartments. People discouraged, having to pick up the pieces again.

If I'd stayed on in Lebanon just a little bit longer, I would have been with them. Instead, safe at home, the radiator hot, the tea kettle whistling, I allowed myself one more luxury. To feel cheated of experience, cheated of the story—Evelyn under Fire—that might have been mine.

LESSONS

In Hamra, I am introduced to my cousin Wadad. At 70 or thereabouts, she is beautiful still. Radiant, in fact. Widowed young, she has spent decades teaching the blind and deaf. "They are my life," she says. In Texas, her three grown children, who have fled the war, volunteer their time to work with prison inmates. Bring them the word of God. Wadad is pious too, but unconventional. As a young woman, she studied for a year in Massachusetts. Then planned to travel the long way home, visiting institutions for the blind in Japan, the Philippines, and India. New England was one thing, her father had gone along with that. But this new fancy was too much for him—his daughter on her own in outlandish places with no kin to call on. He told her no. She was still in Boston when word came he had died. Quietly, her brother sent her money for the trek through Asia. That and her mother's blessings.

Her friend and I sit with Wadad in her living room with its low sofas and Palestinian-embroidered cushions. The conversation turns to excursions, first for me, then for the two of them. Wadad leans forward, eyes bright with an idea. To drive south beyond Sidon and Tyre into villages patrolled by soldiers Israel has armed and paid for. "Why not!" she coaxes her friend who smiles a little at her nonsense. Wadad turns to me then, and though she doesn't say a word, I feel our pleasant chat has turned into a test. I want so badly to pass with flying colors. "Count me in," I want to say but I'm afraid to follow her across the line she's crossed. Somehow we got our lessons backwards, Wadad and I. Wasn't it my grandparents who adventured westward, hers who shook their heads and hunkered down at home?

The first time I dropped by to introduce myself, I took Wadad an armful of hothouse flowers. "Oh, let's not start!" she pleaded. I knew what she meant because the immigrants carried it across the seas and taught it to their children, this grammar of formality, this extravagance of gesture. One day, in a café on Hamra Street, two grown men at the table next to me do battle to determine who will pay the check.

"Allow me, my friend."

"No, no, my brother."

"For love of me, I beg you!"

It escalates beyond words. They are pushing, grabbing arms, half rising from their seats, one actually throwing folding money into the other's lap. I recognize the rhetoric and know from the beginning who will win.

Twice a week, I take Arabic lessons at one of the universities. In a shadowy office with no windows, my tutor is a darker shadow yet. A middle-aged woman, always in black, even to shoes and stockings. Her face too is colorless, no makeup ever. She's mourning her husband, who died three years before. "How long were you married?" I finally ask. "Thirty-two years," she tells me, "and, believe me, every minute was sweet as paradise." I try telling her how lucky she is, but she doesn't want to hear it. Looking at her, you'd think she was panting after death. But one day, in the middle of a lesson, the sound of an explosion startles us.

She goes very still.

Terrified it's all about to start again.

From the first, I tell her that I know some Arabic. But the information doesn't take. We start with the definite article, lesson 1 in a beginners' textbook. At the end of the session, I tell her again. She smiles, and assigns lesson 2. I spend the rest of the term avoiding tenses I'm not supposed to know yet and idioms she hasn't introduced me to.

My best lessons come from Bilal, also, as it happens, twice a week, the two afternoons he chauffeurs me to and from my class 45 minutes from Beirut. On our first trip, he is unsure of the road and so am I, though I have been this way before. But we keep climbing in hairpin turns and arrive at last. Gabbing all the way, which is astonishing since he knows no English, except "hello" and "thank you." Later, I will teach him to ask, "Where to?" and "How are you today?" I learn to say, "Keef?" [how?] when he goes too fast for me in my parents' tongue. But he repeats, is patient. Pieces together my broken Arabic and conjures out my meaning. "Very good," he tells me. "Anyone can understand you." One day, there's a change in plans; a colleague drives me to campus and back. The next time I see Bilal, I try to explain, groping for words. "What's happened to your Arabic?" he demands. "We lose one day and you go backwards." He's telling me he missed me.

We talk about everything: the traffic, my students, cancer, school-yard killings in the States, the Lebanese prime minister. I report on a party at the American embassy; he fills me in on his brother who is prospering in Germany. "But I stay here," he says and it sounds final. Whenever he can work it into the conversation, he brags about his little girl, who is smart in school. ("I wish she will be a doctora like you.") About his wife, El-Madame, who has studied English. One day he hands me, proudly, her recipe for lentil soup, written in a careful hand he cannot read a word of. "Correct?" he asks, meaning her English. "Perfect," I say.

The holidays approach, his and mine. I rejoice that no one will expect Christmas cards from me this year. Meanwhile, Bilal fasts—for a month, sunrise to sunset, no food, not a sip of water—and expounds on verses from the Holy Koran, studying me through the rearview mirror, watching my eyes. "We deny ourselves," he explains, "to feel what the poor and hungry suffer. To soften our hearts toward the afflicted." I love to hear him preach. Find in his words the same comfort I feel at five in the morning, when I wake to the muezzin calling the faithful to prayer. The solace of a human voice. At dusk, Bilal and I drive home along Hamra Street, under a bower of streamers that spell out "MERRY CHRISTMAS, BLESSED RAMADAN" in Arabic and English.

Our last day together, I give Bilal an extra tip and a box tied with gold ribbon. Chocolates for the children, I tell him, and for El-Madame. He blushes, the first time I've seen him at a loss for words. Eighteen months later, I turn up again, and Bilal drives me to campus once more, so I can visit with my students. All the way, he and I are like an old married couple, looking back on the milestones of our courtship.

"Remember that tall house?" he says. "When you saw it, you said we were on the right road."

"Yes, yes, I remember."

"Look there, the garage where I asked the mechanic for directions."

"Yes, you called him 'professor.'"

Bilal is delighted. "You remember that!"

MY LEBANESE STUDENTS

When I'm on sabbatical from my regular teaching, the last place I want to find myself is in another classroom. But one course that met for under two hours, and just twice a week: how bad could that be? What I didn't count on was being smitten by my students.

They were third-year English majors, studying not at either of the elite and private American universities, but at the publicly funded Lebanese University. Poorly funded, as it turned out. Very poorly. My branch was outside Beirut, set on a rise with a lovely view of city and sea. But the dilapidated complex that held classrooms and offices was not lovely. And, though once a monastery, was hardly picturesque. Inside, chipped stairs, cracked walls, dingy windows, and toilets that occasionally flushed. Outside, one basketball hoop and a tattered ping-pong table.

I soon discovered that things I'd taken for granted at home didn't exist. An office of my own, access to a computer, a reliable phone line. Even paper for the photocopy machine. "We get one package a month," the secretary told me. And repeated it when I couldn't believe I'd heard her right.

And yet this was a place where education was carried on with energy and rigor. At home, year after year, seasoned classics were leached out of the curriculum, deemed too hard or too irrelevant. For my Lebanese students, English was a second language, sometimes a third. Yet they read Shakespeare, Chaucer, the Romantics, and seemed both able to cope and not unhappy about it. In my class they read American literature, almost none of it contemporary. But that didn't mean they couldn't connect.

"Oh, doctor, I read the story. It was so sad. Like a knife in my heart!"

This was not a rhetoric I was used to. And though mannered and perhaps even calculated, it was also charming. As was the students' lack of griping about grades. "Fifty is passing," the chair told me. "No one gets over 90, a few perhaps in the eighties or perhaps not; with scores in the seventies they will be very happy; in the sixties they will be quite satisfied."

"Oh, doctor, I want so much to do well on your test. So you will not think we are stupid in Lebanon."

※

"Doctor, are you proud of being Lebanese?" She had caught me off guard. I felt on the spot, all eyes in the class watching me. "Oh yes," I said, dredging up old anodynes about the beauty of the mountains, the hospitality of the people, the love of family. She didn't look satisfied. I piled on vineyards and olive groves, and spectacular grottos. Still, she wasn't buying. Desperate, I threw in Phoenician forbears, Crusader castles, and Roman temples. "Have I answered your question?" I said. What I meant was, "Have I proved I'm on your side?"

After class, she put me in my patronizing place. "Don't you know about the war?" She spoke rapidly, fingers bending and unbending the corner of her notebook. "Muslims and Christians and Druze all killing each other. How can you be proud?"

On another day, a young woman, whom I knew to be Christian, was eager to tell us a story. "Doctor, two years ago I was struck by the Evil Eye. I had the mark of an eye on my arm"—she indicated the spot—"and no medicine could heal it."

"It's all in your mind," sneered a young man. The class looked from him to her; they'd never been so attentive.

"No, no," she insisted, twisting around in her chair. "It was really the Evil Eye, not even the priest could help me."

"What happened?" asked several voices.

"My family bought medicine from an old Druze lady and I drank it." She paused, milking the moment, and then announced, "The mark disappeared the next day!" The class was spellbound, not wanting to believe, and yet . . . . And then another young man spoke up.

"I am Druze," he said, and we gave him our full attention. "Some of our people," he said, "have the same beliefs. But they get their medicine from an old Christian woman."

The class erupted in laughter. More moments like that, I thought, and there would be no fighting to shame us.

※

"Doctor, are you coming to our party?" It was November 22, assassination day to Americans; but to the Lebanese, the anniversary of their independence. In the auditorium, students and faculty were sitting and standing and milling around. From the stage, patriotic songs were sung, dances danced, poems recited. One statuesque young woman gave a long, impassioned speech, her hands, like a diva's, clasped in front of her chest, her head thrown back in defiance. After almost every sentence, the audience cheered and applauded and she stamped her foot. Young men linked arms and broke into dance. It was old-fashioned patriotism, it was old-time religion. Impossible to imagine at home.

But then, I reflected, the United States was not a country under foreign occupation.

Most of the classical Arabic from the stage was beyond me. But even I could hear the keening over Lebanon, the dirge for Beirut, the longing for a day when the Lebanese could move freely through all the rooms of their house. In the south, Lebanese territory was still under Israeli control. Through my classroom window, I had a view of Syrian soldiers hanging out their laundry.

"Oh, doctor, it is wrong to hate, I know. But these soldiers?" The young woman's voice dropped to a whisper. "I feel I could kill them."

✖

"Doctor, America is a democracy. Why do they treat the black people so cruelly? Why did they kill the Indians?" No matter which way you turned those questions, there were no answers that did Americans proud.

"Doctor, do Americans hate Arabs? Do they think everyone one of us is a terrorist?" For my students, these were not abstract queries. They all had someone—relative or close friend—in the United States. And some in the class were trying to imagine a life for themselves there.

They pointed to social pressures and to lack of opportunity in Lebanon—jobs hard to find, low wages.

"If I could take my friends and family with me," one young man announced, "I would get on the plane tomorrow."

"In America," chimed in his friend, "a man can get what he works hard for, and he can live without fear."

For these young people who had known nothing but war for the first decade of their lives, and intermittent bombing since, fear has a very specific meaning.

"Some say that I am a coward," said a young woman whose house had come within meters of being hit by a bomb. "They say I should stay and defend my country and even die for its sake. But I do not want to die."

"I wish there would be no more war," said another. She was the class cutup. I'd never seen her so wistful, so melancholy. "Then I would not leave, not for wealth or education, or anything, because, do you know, doctor? I cannot spend even one day without seeing my little cousins."

"We should not leave," pleaded an older woman in the class. "We have held on for 20 years, we can hold on a few more. We must give our country a chance."

"But if I am ever obliged to leave," came a voice from the back, "I will live always in hope of returning to Lebanon."

"I can understand that," I said. And the whole classroom nodded.

Lebanon was a natural fit. On the other hand, left to my own devices, I would not have made a beeline for the Arabian Peninsula. Except for a couple of the larger states, it was all a blur to me, one emirate, kingdom, or sultanate shading into another. But, like a number of American colleges and universities, the one at which I taught had decided to offer a degree program in the Gulf. Such arrangements were to each party's benefit. They made money for the American schools (more students, more tuition) and also conferred panache (it was classy to have an international footprint). For their part, the Gulf nations gained a well honed curriculum, access to a seasoned pool of instructors, and, for their students, an American degree. Given too the conservative values of families in that region, it was no small matter that daughters could gain many of the benefits of an American education while still living at home under the protection of parents and older siblings.

Bahrain was the country my college struck a deal with. According to its terms, we offered a series of intensive courses, usually just three weeks long, taught in succession. Each theoretically (though, of course, not actually) the equivalent of a normal one-semester course. Selected American faculty went overseas, taught a single course, and returned. I'd anticipated stiff competition for these plum teaching slots, which carried advantages in terms of both salary and work load as well as a quick dip into a patently exotic culture. And, since each course was over in a flash, it would hardly interfere with an instructor's other obligations; spouse and children would have little cause to complain. My only hope was that when decisions were being made about whom to send, my background would argue in my favor. I needn't have been concerned. Most of my fellow faculty were convinced that the patch of map colored "Arab" was one extended battlefield. Thanks, but they would rather stay at home.

Foolish of them, I thought. The college administration, cautious by nature, would not be sending us into a danger zone. Though in getting to Bahrain we did come close: on the in-flight screens that tracked our route across Europe and the Middle East, I watched our plane swing off course in order to skirt skies over Iraq. Of course, in a country like Bahrain, ruled by a religious minority, chary of political freedoms, and to top it off home to an American naval base, the potential for violence cannot be dismissed out of hand. Thus, American sailors are advised not to congregate in groups in restaurants and other public places, and, at the gate to the ritziest hotel in town, guards halt all cars and search their trunks, presumably not just for the fun of it. Still, except perhaps for East Asian women working as domestics, Bahrain has, so far, been a safe foreign destination.

By the time I arrived, the program had been underway for a year. Which meant that we faculty went over in pairs in order to accommodate both freshmen and in my case sophomores. Housed on the executive floor of a hotel overlooking the Gulf, we were pampered in a manner to which I, for one, was not accustomed. In the business alcove off the executive lounge, I would no sooner pull up to a computer than a smiling someone would appear to offer tea or coffee. In the dining room, the staff was attentive to a fault: my plate whisked away almost before I'd forked the last baby okra or sopped up the last of the tomato gravy, my coffee cup topped off when it was down an inch, ditto for my water tumbler. If I visited the buffet table for another helping of olives or cheese, I'd come back to find my napkin neatly re-folded at my place. It was too much. Instead of feeling grateful or assuming such service was my due, I grew increasingly annoyed. "Back off," I wanted to say, but, of course, if they did they could lose their jobs.

It may have been the sense of being watched that got to me. Or the embarrassment at playing "have" to someone else's "have-not." And what many things come down to, I knew my mother would not approve. On the rare occasions when she agreed to have someone in to clean house, she pitched right in: unthinkable for her to sit idle while another woman scrubbed her bathtub or mopped her kitchen floor. My sensitivities are not that nice—my cleaning woman comes in every other week and does her work without any help from me. (Or any supervision either, because I'm not yet convinced that I have the right to ask her to do this or not do that.) But the babying at the hotel was in a different league. And much of it, I may as well confess, was welcome. Nothing wrong with fresh flowers in my room, or dark chocolates, or a bowl of constantly replenished fruit.

My college footed the bill. All living and travel expenses were covered, including incidentals like phone calls home and laundry. (Only when it came to hairdressers, as I discovered, did the accountants draw the line.) But the longer I and my colleague were in the country, the more we found ourselves reaching for our personal credit cards or rummaging in purse or pocket for our private hoard of cash. At a minimum, a few coins for charity if one had a bent in that direction. Beggars sat cross-legged on the sidewalks, silent, dignified, and secure in the knowledge that they were a blessing to the faithful since giving alms to the poor is one of the five pillars of Islam. "You're a good Muslim," I teased my colleague after he'd dropped a coin in one beggar's hand. "I'm a good *person*," he said, managing to make me feel, at once, niggardly and provincial. But mostly we spent money in the shops. Though I'd promised myself I'd buy only a few souvenirs, I came home with a gold pendant, a rope of tiny sapphires (admittedly, not high-grade), and a 9'-by-12' Oriental rug, as well as a dozen miniature rugs useful as placemats and, it turned out, as conversation pieces. Add to all that the batch of inlaid boxes and small woven hangings that I gave away to family and neighbors.

The rugs came from shops downtown, the weavings from a national crafts center, but most of my other purchases were items I picked up in the *souk*. Whether I and my colleague were out to buy or just to look around, we never tired of its attractions—black-garbed women on the street, tucking their hair into their scarves as they hurried their children along; old men in thobes to the ankle and stout sandals leaning on one another's arms; tailors and shoemakers hunched in their cubbyholes; merchants squatting beside pyramids of spices and fat sacks of nuts, dried fruit, and grains. Also—this was a tourist magnet, after all—wares designed to catch the eye of foreigners. Things like papier mâché bangles (charming and cheap, you could buy them by the armful), incense burners with crenellated eaves, model dhows that called to mind the fishing fleet I could see from my hotel window, framed verses from the Koran in elaborate Arabic calligraphy, brass trays and the intricate camel-head stands (each carved from a single log of wood) that turned trays into tables, 24-carat-gold chains at hard-to-beat prices.

One day, the *souk* was stage to a spectacle that went beyond the ordinary. It was Ashura, when Shiites mourn the Prophet Mohammed's grandson, Hussain, who was martyred outside Karbala (in what is now Iraq), together with his entire family. Mourn him and look back with dismay on the failure of his allies to support him and on the galling victory of power and privilege over justice. On Ashura, as if to keep the wound of their sorrow raw, Shiites traditionally scourge themselves with chains and slash themselves with swords. In Bahrain, such self-mutilation has been outlawed (though

Evelyn Shakir

I saw evidence of it in heads wrapped with blood-stained rags). Instead, processions of men and boys march in orderly rank though the old city, chanting prayers, and—in synchronized motion— swinging small chains, which can't do much damage, against their chest and back. The hotel staff had advised us to stay out of the *souk* that day, but my colleague and I didn't want to pass up what might be our only chance to witness the ritual. I wrapped my hair in a dark scarf I'd picked up on purpose; he, lean and tanned, easily mistaken for a local, needed no special camouflage. Still, he was intent on keeping a low profile, more for my sake perhaps than for his own, and kept coaxing me to the back of the crowd that lined the narrow streets. Stubbornly, I kept darting forward. Mistake, I thought, as a man turned, looked at me, looked at my camera. Then—to my relief—smiled and made way for me.

Ashura and all the piety it implies was one face of Bahrain. But there was another. Late on Wednesday, the last day of the Saudi Arabian work week, well-heeled Saudi men (some with their wives) would leave their homes to drive across the causeway to Bahrain's capital, Manama. All weekend, hotels like mine were full, and the streets congested with cars bearing Saudi plates. For these birds of passage, Manama was a playground. Women could walk about or even drive about on their own, with their faces showing or, if they wanted, in T-shirts and jeans. Alcohol was served in restaurants and hotels. (My own hotel had a Happy Hour each afternoon.) Sexual adventuring was easier; some of those Saudi men had mistresses or what amounted to second wives installed in Manama.

The two faces of Bahrain were epitomized for me in the view I had of the hotel swimming pool. I watched waiters carry lunch plates out to hotel guests—often airline pilots and hostesses— who'd been swimming laps and were now sunning themselves in lounge chairs. What did the staff think, I wondered, of the Western women in skimpy bikinis, totally at their ease, apparently oblivious to the possibility that they were offending local sensibilities. It could not have been more stark, the contrast between that half-naked crowd and the Arab women who occasionally showed up at the pool with hardly a square inch of skin exposed. I remember one, in particular. While her husband and little boy frolicked in the water, cooling off on a very hot day, she positioned herself in the shade of the building for whatever relief it could provide.

I had come to Bahrain with no particular animus against the long black *abaya* that most Bahraini women wear on the street or even against the curtain-like veil behind which many hide their faces. Live and let live. After all, I reasoned, when it came to dress and female modesty, most societies drew the line somewhere. (Wouldn't an American woman who appeared in public nude to the waist land in trouble with the law?) But, as the days passed and I saw one Bahraini woman after another, her hands gloved, her face layered with fabric, strolling along the seaside beside her bare-headed husband in comfortable slacks and open-collared shirt, I couldn't help it, I grew indignant. What went on between them I couldn't say and was not my business. But it was hard to miss the implicit assertion of patriarchal rights—the man's wife was his property and his alone to gaze at. Call it keeping the upper hand.

After my first stint in Bahrain, I went back twice for repeat performances. Each time, the streets were more choked with cars, the pace of construction more frenzied, the skyline dominated by futuristic skyscrapers that had gone up when I wasn't looking. But the hotel felt like home, and the staff remembered me. On my second visit, one Nepalese waiter showed me the photo of his infant boy whom he had never seen in the flesh; only once every two years are he and his colleagues *allowed* vacations long enough to *allow* them to go home. I still meandered in the *souk* but didn't splurge. At lunch in the hotel, I still gorged on *Um Ali*, a warm pudding of bread, cream, nuts, and raisins; when I said my final good-bye to the maitre d', he gave me the recipe. At the end of my most recent trip, I tacked on a few days in Oman, where I visited Job's Tomb, waited in a cab while camels (regal as sultans) made their unhurried way across the road, watched milky white frankincense ooze from trees, and floated on my back in the Indian Ocean.

All the same, when I hear someone speak of "the Gulf," it's always that first visit to Bahrain that comes to mind, and that first classroom of students.

Teaching Arab-American Literature in Bahrain

Lebanese immigrants used to tell the story of the man, one of their own, who returned home from the wedding of an American friend and asked if there was anything in the house to eat.

"Didn't they serve food at the wedding?" he was asked.

"Oh, yes, it was a feast."

"Then why are you hungry?"

"Because I didn't eat."

"In the name of God, why not?"

"They didn't insist."

Like most good jokes, it brings home a truth—in this case, that people get along best when they work from the same cultural script and understand the roles they've been assigned. If those conditions had held (both parties being Arab), the host would have pressed food on his guest, piling his plate high; he would not have taken no for an answer. The guest, his reluctance proving it wasn't a free meal he was after, would at last have relented and eaten his fill. Both would have shown themselves to be men of good breeding.

Here's what it sounds like when it's done right. In a scene from Rabih Almeddine's novel *Koolaids*, a Lebanese-American artist by the name of Mohammad has just offered a work to the narrator and his lover.

"This is very generous, but we can't take it."

. . . "I will hear none of it," Mohammad said. "This is now your painting."

. . . "We don't deserve it."

"Nonsense. I wouldn't have it any other way."

"This is too much."

"Do not disgrace me by refusing my gift."

"Thank you so much," I said. "I will place it in the most honored place in my house."

When Arab Americans read this passage or hear the joke about the wedding guest, we immediately recognize what is going on. Scenes from our past crowd in on us. Our whole lives have prepared us to understand. And part of the pleasure of getting the point is the conviction of its being denied—in a full-bodied way—to outsiders. The laughter in our throats says we belong.

When I agreed to teach a three-week "intensive" in Bahrain, I thought I would offer my students that same satisfaction by focusing the class on Arab-American literature. Here were characters they would recognize; cultural mandates they would immediately *get*. I embarked on this project with some confidence. As a person of Arab background, I would understand—even share—my students' cultural instincts. For their part, they would be pleased to be taught by one of their own.

It didn't take long for my assumptions to be called into question. For one thing, although my students and I got along fine, it didn't follow that they saw me as one of *their people*.

CLASS DISCUSSION

The question of my identity arose on the very first day of class, as we were discussing a poem by the Palestinian-born writer Fawaz Turki. "Being a Good *Americani*" is about a man engaged in suburban rituals—painting the kitchen table, driving to 7-Eleven for beer, trading conjectures about who shot JR, scolding his son for playing with his genitals. But the role doesn't take. When he speaks of his blond wife, his "American family," and his haunting memories of Palestine, it's clear that, for all his efforts to fit in, he does not feel like a "good *Americani*." Perhaps, in fact—as some students argued—he does not even feel of one family with his wife and his son.

We parsed Turki's portrait of a good American, its satiric take, its underlying melancholy, its refusal to defer to the high-flown myths through which Americans prefer to define themselves. In the midst of this hammering out, I told about a student in the States who'd once informed me that naturalized citizens—whatever the law said—were not real Americans. "Do you mean," I'd asked him, "that only native-born Americans are *real*?" "No," he'd said, "that's not enough. The parents and grandparents also have to be born here." "But," I'd persisted, thinking to shame him, "my parents were not born in this country. So I'm not a real American?" "That's right," he'd said.

By now, I'd repeated this story to any number of friends and colleagues, all of whom had rolled their eyes or shaken their heads. From my Bahraini students, I expected a similar or stronger response. We would stand shoulder to shoulder against xenophobia. My only fear was that I was taking too cheap a shot; not all Americans are like that student, I kept repeating. The class just stared. Appalled, I thought. Until a young man at the back in a snow white thobe and checkered headdress set me straight. Salman understood perfectly my former student's point of view. Substitute "Bahraini" for "American," he said, and he would feel the same. Several generations in his country did not seem an unreasonable prerequisite for citizenship, much less full acceptance. And, even then, one would have to find out why the "newcomer" wanted to be Bahraini—for selfish reasons or in order to contribute to the welfare of the country.

It was the first of several times, my Bahraini students caught me off guard, exploding my expectations, delineating the gulf that lay between their views and mine. But also prompting me to re-examine my assumptions. Perhaps in a tiny island kingdom, where families have lived for centuries and identity has traditionally been synonymous with tribe and clan, claims to belong must be weighed on a different scale.

Still, I wasn't ready to let the matter drop. "As you know," I said, "my parents were immigrants, but I feel as American as anyone else."

"Oh, yes"—many voices spoke up at once—"you *are* American."

Perhaps they meant to reassure me. Their intentions, I think, were not unkind. But it was their certainty that got to me. *No possibility of taking you for one of us*, they seemed to say. Shut out, put in my place. What was it that set me so decisively apart?

One answer was religion. My students were Muslim; my heritage was Christian. More important, my connection to the church was a matter of sentiment and aesthetics rather than belief. Even my parents had seldom attended services. But Islam was central to my students' lives. (Most girls in the class wore black *abayas*, covered their hair with scarves, and didn't fool with makeup.) Piety was the context they brought to everything. Had I been a person of strong faith, though a faith not their own, we would have been closer kin. (In one of my classes at home, the students who most often saw eye to eye were two girls: the first, a Pakistani Muslim who wore long sleeves and a scarf; the other, the daughter of Evangelical Christian missionaries.)

Not that the difference in our religious background or the temperature of our faith ever became a topic of discussion. Delicacy on their part, perhaps, and on mine a sense that Arab culture cut across religious lines.

Still, I was conscious enough of religion to make sure a patently "Muslim" poem was among the earliest work we read. The writer was

Sam Hamod; the poem was "After the Funeral of Assam Hamady," in which the poet recalls driving across South Dakota, as a young man, bringing his grandfather, father, and father's friend back from a funeral in Iowa. Suddenly the grandfather grabs Hamod's arm and commands him to stop the car. "It's time to pray," he decrees, pulling out a Navajo blanket. By the side of the highway, the three older men kneel as cars whiz by and strangers gawk. Despite being urged, "Get over here to pray!" Hamod refuses. Too embarrassed. Instead, he offers to "stand guard." At the end, the poem shifts years ahead to a present moment saturated with regret.

> . . . *I am standing here now*
> *Trying so hard to join them*
> *On that old prayer blanket—*
> *As if the pain behind my eyes*
> *Could be absolution.*

To me, a striking feature of the poem had always been the way Hamod devotes line after line to the Muslim prayer the three men chant. Not in translation, which would be one thing, but simply transliterated and thus gibberish to most English-speaking readers. Expiation, I suggested. The man who was too embarrassed to pray in front of Americans back then is praying now. Heedless of appearing freakish.

My students consented to all that—or, at least, did not object—but something else was foremost on their minds. "The prayer is not right," they told me. I hadn't known that. Yes, they said, phrases were garbled, the sequence of lines confused. I thanked them for the information, but they were unwilling to move on. It was a serious matter, to alter the words of the Koran. A sin, in fact. "See what happens in America?" one said.

Only then did I realize that to my students, my carefully chosen "Muslim" poem was about religion in a sense more deep than I'd imagined. Their major concern was that their faith be properly represented. Such personal considerations as the poet's state of mind were secondary. His regret, in fact, rang hollow if he could be so sloppy. And he'd fallen down in other respects as well. Referred to important matters but not explained them—for instance why certain rites are performed—"They rub their hands / Then their faces," and why the men face East when praying. How mean of him, incidentally, not to help his elders out when he sees they've miscalculated and are facing "what must surely be South." To top it off, one girl said, the premise of the poem was wrong. Islam did not require that one pray at a particular hour when it was so clearly inconvenient. They should have waited until they were home.

And then from the same student—I came to think of Nayla as my *contrarian*—what seemed to me an egregious misreading that made nonsense of the poem. She argued that the poet was genuinely worried when he said he'd stand guard as the others prayed. But even his father doesn't buy that, I said. Look at what he says—"Guard from what?" "No," she insisted, "Americans hate Arabs so much, you don't know what might happen." Clearly, class discussion had shot off in directions I hadn't intended or foreseen.

It seems to me now, as I look back on that day, that the roles of student and teacher kept turning inside out and back again, like the cupped hands of an Arab woman dancing. I was the designated expert on literature; but they had it all over me when it came to Islam. That was fine. I was eager to learn about their faith and, even more so, about how they processed this or any piece of literature.

Also, as it happened, the poem itself was about teaching—and missed opportunities. Or so my students thought. They blamed the father for the son's ignorance, hanging their indictment on one sentence in the poem: "My father says to the others: 'He's foolish, he doesn't know how / to pray.'" Well, whose fault was that, they demanded? The father's, of course, a fault analogous to the son's failure to teach his readers properly (or, for that matter, to correct his companions about the direction in which they were praying). Poor teaching was being modeled in the poem. In our classroom we were trying to do better. But, though we didn't call each other "foolish," we met with only mixed results. I don't know that I ever convinced some students that the impulse of the poem was not didactic, much less that poetry is not religious tract. Nor, for my part, could I follow with easy conscience the path that they were blazing.

Still, their reading served to remind me that meaning grows out of choices—what to foreground and what to give short shrift—decisions dictated by what one brings to the table to begin with. Critical jargon would have it that my students *de-familiarized* the text for me, or *complicated* it. In doing so, they inevitably enriched it. I was forced, for instance, to take into account the mangling of prayer that loomed so large for them although I could not agree that, in itself, it was evidence of moral failing. I was beguiled too by the proposition they implicitly laid out—that all of us, the cast of characters in both the classroom and the poem, were implicated in a web of mutual responsibilities. Reading (like writing, teaching, or parenting) was not a game.

As we progressed through the term, I did a balancing act between keeping an open mind and remaining true to my own understanding of any given text. I reminded myself that what felt to me like distortion was, for my students—sometimes—a matter of deep conviction. I felt too that the attentiveness with which they approached the literature (putting my American students to shame) earned them the right to be listened to with respect. Nor could I deny that our give and take was making me, for better or worse, a more cautious reader.

A case in point: "Holy Toledo," a short story by the Lebanese-American writer Joseph Geha. Set in Chicago, it centers on 11-year-old Nadia, her younger brother Mikhi, their grandmother, and their uncle, the four of whom have lived together since the children's widowed father more or less dumped his offspring on his mother's doorstep. The house they live in is dark, cluttered, musty, an emblem of narrow, old-world thinking and suffocating family ties. In keeping with that atmosphere, the grandmother (in Arabic, *sitti*) controls the children by frightening them into thinking that at any moment she may have a heart attack and die. The uncle, in the old days "quick to laugh," is now a harsh disciplinarian, regularly pulling off his snakeskin belt to lay into Mikhi and, less often, Nadia at the merest sign of disrespect. Instead of protecting her grandchildren, *sitti*—at a climactic moment in the story—eggs her son on. But, even as the uncle prepares to apply the belt again—to Mikhi because *sitti* accuses him of blasting her with his Evil Eye, to Nadia for daring to defend him—Nadia determines to run away with her brother, leaving the Lebanese enclave in which they live and seeking out "America," the same America to which their father has already made his escape.

The story calls to mind folk tales in which children fall into the hands of ogres and wicked witches. But the father seems a different sort, more fed up than anything, someone whom the children miss but toward whom they seem to harbor no resentment, perhaps because, like Hansel and Gretel's parents, he is less immediately present in the story.

Or so I would have said. But for most of my Bahraini students, he *was* the story. Yes, the grandmother was unloving; and yes, the uncle may have gone a bit too far; but it was the father whose behavior was unforgivable, shunting his responsibilities onto others, abandoning his own children. I had approached the story as quasi-allegory, the father and uncle—two second-generation sons—deliberately constructed to represent alternatives: staying home or striking out, belonging or autonomy, the comfort of the familiar or the challenge of independent thinking. Whatever the choice, I'd argued, there was a price to pay. In the father's case, for instance, "a vicious homesickness."

My explication cut no ice with them. What choice did the uncle have, they asked—forced to care for his brothers' children and to put his own dreams on hold. For me to point out that the story neither delineates such dreams (though the souring of his disposition does point to frustration) nor invites us to dwell for long on the father's dereliction of duty—in fact is halfway sympathetic to his urge to flee—all this persuaded no one. They would not let Geha (any more than Hamod) pull the wool over their eyes or make them lose their moral bearings. Even at the cost, in this case, of glossing over physical abuse. The uncle was not such a bad fellow, they told me. At least, he tried to teach the children right from wrong.

As for *sitti* and the Evil Eye, no need, at all, to gloss that over. Fear of the "hot eye" was only natural, several students said. Did they too believe? Those who spoke up said *yes*. Not just believed, it turned out, but could name names of individuals whose jealous gaze could blight a healthy fruit tree or a beautiful child. "You know who I mean," one girl in Western dress said to another. A third girl, whom I'd pegged as the most devout in the class, insisted that Scripture confirmed the existence of the Evil Eye. "Show me," I said. Next class, she brought in a copy of the Koran and directed me to the relevant passage, which turned out to be only a general warning against envious people. I didn't argue the point, at least not very hard. But to think, as *sitti* did, that an amulet would protect you—yes, that part was superstition. Only prayer would avail.

I could not go all the way with my students (certainly not in their riffs on the Evil Eye), but I could see they had a point. After all, whose fault was it that the children had landed in this house and in these hands? As the daughter of immigrants myself, I'd been caught up in typical second-generation issues—chief among them, the pull of home vs. the seduction of the world beyond that horizon. But in Bahrain, where faith and family were one, the sacred duty of parent to child and of child to parent was always what it was all about.

As I found out again when we approached another of Geha's stories. "Everything, Everything" centers on a battle of wills between a young woman and her immigrant mother. At issue is Barbara's desire for a zone of privacy, represented by the glove compartment of her car, which her mother keeps pressing her to open. The more the daughter refuses, the more suspicious her mother becomes. "Something you don' wan' me to see him?" Soon the mother's intrusiveness becomes unbearable.

Barbara wanted only a little quiet, like the hush the tires were making on the wet pavement—shh, shh.

"Shh, Beebee? Howse come you say that?"
"My God, I'm just breathing."
"Howse come you breat'ing shh?"
"I don't know, can't I breathe?"

This mother's style is not to rant. She prefers to play the martyr. In response to Barbara's claim that there is "nothing" in the glove compartment, the older woman arranges herself, "arms folded over her purse in a hunched posture that says 'Lies, too, I bear as Christ bore the cross.'"

Though different in her personality, Barbara's mother, it seemed to me, was sister under the skin to *sitti*. Both of them manipulative, determined, self-pitying. "What do these two women have in common?" I'd asked the students to think about that before they came to class. The answer most brought back was "Nothing." Unlike *sitti*, they told me, Barbara's mother cared. Wasn't she too insistent, I suggested. Not at all, they said. She was acting as a good mother should, seeking to know everything about her daughter so that she could protect and guide her. By the same token, for a daughter to keep secrets from her mother or try to shut her out was wrong.

A single voice dissented. Inea hated the way her own mother had to know everything. "I tell Aysha"—she nodded at her cousin—"you talk too much. You don't have to go home and tell our mothers what we had for lunch." (Here was news. Demure Aysha, who never said

76

a word in class, a chatterbox.) "I pick one thing to tell my mother so she doesn't get on me," Inea said. "Then I think, *There! That should hold her for a week.*" Of course, she was the girl who'd said from the beginning, "This place is not for me."

The last and longest text we read was *West of the Jordan*, a novel that features four female teenage cousins, three of them in the United States and one still back in Palestine. The author, Leila Halaby, has situated them along a continuum from acquiescence to rebellion. At one extreme is Mawal, the girl who has never left her village and seems destined to replicate her mother's life; at the other extreme is Saroya, who secretly defies her parents by changing into tight clothes after she leaves the house, dancing provocatively, and sleeping with men.

From the start, in order to focus my students' attention, I'd asked them to select one cousin and track her through the book. We came together after they had read the opening chapters. "Okay," I said, "who did you choose?" Each of the four cousins had been singled out by someone, but the name I heard most often was Saroya. The sexpot. "Foiled again," I thought. "What's going on here?" I said.

Well, of course, they didn't approve of her behavior. Everyone agreed on that. Still, to a plurality of my students, she was the most interesting. She had fire, they said. She made them want to read on. "And what about Mawal?" I asked. I put the case for her: she was a good girl, stable, kind, seemingly at peace with herself. "She's boring!" they said. Their allegiance to Saroya was put to the test later in the book when they discovered she had slept with her uncle. The condemnation was universal. "That's disgusting!" "That's too much!" "I felt it couldn't be what I was thinking." Some regretted they'd ever paid her the compliment of selecting her for special attention. "I'd like to shoot her," one said. But almost at once she began backtracking. Five minutes into class, she declared that Saroya was "still the most interesting."

I didn't understand it then, and I'm not sure I fully understand it now. Except to note that they found her some moral wriggle room—she would not have been so wild, so un-Muslim, they said, if her parents had done better by her, paid her more attention. No matter what texts we read, we never seemed to move far from the mantra of parental responsibility. That loophole aside, the truth is that my students—those who chose her—were apparently drawn to her, as they said, because she seemed the liveliest, the hungriest for life. But also, I suspect, because she spoke to whatever spark of naughtiness they were harboring in their own breasts—and, I think, whatever sexual curiosity or urgings. Hamod, Barbara, even Nadia and her brother—not to mention the other three girls in the novel—none of them had seduced those students who would turn out to be Saroya's hard-core fans; with none of them had they identified. It took an out-and-out rebel to engage them.

FINAL ESSAY

So far, in speaking of my students' reactions, I have drawn only on class discussion, and, as is almost always true, that give-and-take was dominated by certain voices. Which made it difficult to know with certainty what the quieter students thought—some never said a word unless personally invited to, and even then a couple were too shy to do more than smile. The daily written assignments did provide clues. But it was the final essays—more detailed and comprehensive—that gave me my best sense of each student's thinking and that offered a last chance for dissenting voices to be heard. For instance, on the matter of the Evil Eye. My student Mohammed wrote that belief in it was "crazy and irrational." Bashful Aysha, who dressed in the traditional *abaya*, didn't go quite that far. But she did suspect that blaming the "hot eye" might just be a rationale to explain away misfortune.

In preparation for writing their essays, my students had met with me in my office, coming in before class or staying late, asking for guidance, testing approaches. On days class wasn't held, they had come to my hotel, first drafts in hand. With just a few days to go, they'd put everything they had into it. Back home in Boston again, I read the final drafts and was impressed. These were not the hurried, patchwork efforts my American students too often handed in at semester's end, as if they'd run out of energy about a week too soon or had more important courses to attend to. Though, to be fair, in Bahrain the students took only one course at a time. On the other hand, each course ran for just three short weeks, and we were nearly two weeks in before topics were assigned.

Of the two that proved most popular, one asked students to write a letter to a person of their choosing. "Make it someone," I said, "who you think would profit from the readings in this course." A third of my students took on this challenge, two of them using it as an opportunity to urge a friend or relative in the United States to return home. By now, the literature had persuaded all my students that immigration—or even long stints abroad—can lead to serious personal and family upheavals, but only these two girls were giving up entirely on the enterprise. In itself, perhaps, not startling except that these were two of only three girls in the class who wore Western clothing—jeans and T-shirts—and they had also spent considerable time abroad. To clinch their arguments, both writers relied on gut-wrenching appeals. "Mom and Dad are growing older," Dalal wrote her brother. . . "I do not want you to end up years from now, as Hamod did, trying so hard to join us on an old prayer blanket." Nayla wrote her sister-in-law, who'd been five years in the States, "It breaks my heart to see your mother keep talking about you as if you were here last week."

And, should her sister-in-law choose to remain in the States, Nayla warned her not to expect her children to learn

> the things that we did when we were young. Things like how
> the younger child has to be the one to serve the older people.

79

Don't be surprised if they don't have time or if they plain "don't want to." Don't expect them to understand the importance of giving you something with their right hand instead of rudely with their left. . . . If they laugh at you when you eat rice with your hand like a cave woman, don't expect them to understand how food is tastier that way.

The other letter writers also addressed themselves to friends or family in the States, not in order to persuade them to return—it seemed a given that they wouldn't or couldn't—but in order to alert them (as Nayla was doing) to trouble ahead. What surprised me— my students' scolding of Hamod, Barbara, and Nadia's delinquent father still ringing in my ears—was the sympathy many essayists expressed for second-generation Arab Americans, caught between the land of their birth or their upbringing and the world out of which their parents came. Yasmine worked it out this way. "As children grow up in America, they feel tempted to do as everyone else around them does. . . . [T]he world they live in is all they know and understand." Such feelings were "understandable." Apparently, the plight of the second-generation was something the students had been silently absorbing all along. Or, more likely, it was the final text, *West of the Jordan*, that had brought them around. Watching four contemporary teenage girls, just a little younger than themselves, struggling with issues of sexuality and marriage, and with parents who, in some cases, were neglectful or worse—that had struck a chord.

Most dramatically in Inea, the class rebel. In an angry outburst of an essay, she declared that daughters of immigrants (like their sisters back home) are practicing schizophrenics, "forced to lead two lives, one in front of family, one in front of friends," and thus, in effect, "taught to be dishonest"; beset on every side by cultural taboos based on a misreading of the Koran; "torn between pursuing their own happiness and pleasing their family and community." Her most daring statement: "Even if Saroya is having sex, she shouldn't have to tiptoe around or be ashamed."

As my student essayists dissected family tensions, they consistently placed the onus of responsibility on the parents. It was their behavior that made all the difference, an analysis consistent with thinking voiced all through the term. A few held that the immigrant generation, if they were patient and trusted in God, might pass on their values intact; others put more emphasis on the wisdom of accommodation. Abdulrahaman, for instance, argued that "change may be a good thing" and that "being American is not a bad thing." (Though he drew the line at behavior expressly forbidden in Islam, such as drinking alcohol or acquiring tattoos.)

And then there were the visionaries—sweet souls—who trusted that, out of the pain of dislocation, something new and wonderful was being forged. "As your ship lowers its anchor on the shores of America," Yasmine apostrophized the immigrants, "think of the new life you are about to create, a life that seems to combine the beauties of two cultures." Mohammed agreed that American-born children "are not Arabs nor American, they are a hybrid of the two." In any case, from generation to generation, change was inevitable. Hadn't Imam Ali, himself, cautioned parents, "Your children were born in a different time than yours, don't force them to do what you used to when you were their age." Those words, Mohammed said, "should be the motto" of the Arab immigrants.

He was the only student to call on tradition in quite that way— that is, to encourage adaptation. But many others, for their different purposes, also drew on cultural or religious authority—sometimes verses from the Koran, sometimes folk tales, sometimes proverbs. As essay after essay wove in such cultural lore, it became clear that doing so was second nature to my students. And that this lore provided a grounding and a context for their lives. I thought of my students back home. It would be most unusual to find one who could or would do the same. Either because they had come to believe that authority was superfluous or because they were orphaned from their communal past.

I remembered one American student—an extreme example I'd like to think—who, in the midst of class discussion, was asked by a classmate what his religious heritage was. He could not answer. He did not know in what religion, if any, he'd been raised. A girl in the class tried to be helpful. "Did you ever make a first communion?" He thought perhaps he had. "Then you're Catholic," she informed him. He didn't argue. In fact, his curiosity was aroused. "Okay," he said, "now what's the difference between a Catholic and a Christian?" I've had people tell me that this is a heartening tale. How wonderful, they've said, that religion and sectarianism have come to mean so little. I guess I don't see it quite that way.

The other topic toward which students gravitated asked them to investigate a question I'd been puzzling over from the start: how did being Muslim shape their reactions to the literature? Once again, it was the conflict between generations that the students zeroed in on—how they as Muslims would judge disputes between parents and children, where their sympathies would lie. The sentiments they expressed echoed what I'd heard voiced in class—for instance, convictions about deference to parents or the prohibition of sexual activity. But what sounded new was the students' ability to get outside their own skins and see the same picture from another point of view. In class, most had seemed more doctrinaire. I tried to think back. Had the voices of the most outspoken students given that particular coloring to class discussion? I thought it went beyond that, but I couldn't say for sure.

In any case more than one essayist was able, in effect, to say, *This is how an American student would read this story; this is how I read it as an Arab or a Muslim; and here's the reason (this value, that priority) for the difference between the two.* I hadn't expected that capacity for detached analysis. As I think about it, it seems to me that their ability to step back and see themselves and others as products of a particular culture is not so different from what's demonstrated in my story about the wedding guest who came home hungry. Though often unschooled and illiterate, immigrants who told that joke at their own expense were already sophisticated enough to realize that their ways were contingent, not inevitable, and self-defeating when carried to an extreme.

Even while acknowledging differences between Arab and American cultures, a number of students sought common ground. Shy Fatima—dressed all in black—wrote that "girls everywhere are the same." Even in Bahrain, she confided, there were a minority who acted like Saroya—wearing skimpy clothes, staying out late, and having sexual intercourse. Aysha simply wrote, "In the end, we are all humans." Such implicit and sometimes explicit advocacy of tolerance was endearing. Take Asma, for instance, the pious girl who had brought me the Koran and to whom quoting scripture came as easily as breathing. She concluded her essay by citing an Islamic adage: "Let's concentrate on the things that are common between us and forgive the differences."

※

Three weeks and 12 class meetings, hours of student conferences, more hours at home reading student essays—where did all that leave me? Certainly not with iron-clad conclusions or luminous epiphanies. But I did learn that my students were a generation at an important crossroads, still deeply embedded in a world where, for all intents and purposes, family, religion, and tradition were one. But also bombarded by alien influences that had left their mark. If nothing else, their curiosity about Saroya told me that.

I learned too that they were right about me. Though we shared certain impulses and traditions, I was not Arab, I was American. It didn't matter finally that I was removed by just one generation from the Arab world, that my dark hair and eyes were Arab, or that I could get by in Arabic. It didn't even matter all that much that I had fashioned a career out of studying Arab-American women and Arab-American literature, had written memoirs about growing up Arab American, had written fiction set in the Arab-American community. As my students had seen, we children of immigrants (and, for that matter, our parents) had built, were building, a culture of our own that was not Arab or not exclusively so. It made more sense to think of it as peculiarly American, an example of what immigrants and their children in this nation of immigrants have always done. The only difference was that, since the ethnic revival of the seventies, we were fashioning our identity more deliberately and more self-consciously. In what now sounds like a dated term, "seeking our roots." Mucking around in the past was the very badge of our American-ness.

Not that I was completely wrong in my early expectation that my Bahraini students and I had important things in common. I too had been taught the primacy of family and its claims over the whims of individuals. And, as a girl, I had also known prohibitions designed to protect me against sexual temptations. Yes, I could dress pretty much as I pleased (although my mother winced at miniskirts and once quietly let down a hem that I promptly took up again), and I could wear makeup (on special occasions, even my mother smeared on a touch of rouge and fluffed on face powder). But as long as I lived at home—that is, until I went away to college—I was not allowed to go out alone on a date. At the age of 21, when I let slip that I had dropped by a man's apartment, my parents could not contain their shock.

But it was the reasoning behind the restrictions that most connected me with my Bahraini students. Reasoning implicitly grounded, perhaps, in religion but made urgent by the most practical social considerations. Shahrazad spelled it out this way: "If Arab people know about a girl that lost her chastity before marriage, they are going to gossip about her, and her reputation will be ruined. No one is going to marry her, and her parents will get the blame." My mother once told me that back home any girl who got "in trouble" would be shunned by the entire village, as would her family. "Oh, we can do without them," the neighbors would say. My mother could never bring herself to issue direct warnings about sex, but she repeated that story to me for a reason.

I grew older, times changed. My father passed on; my mother learned to bend. When I moved into an apartment of my own, she wasn't happy, but she eventually acquiesced, just as she did years later when I took up housekeeping with a man who was not my husband. Little doubt what the villagers would have said, but it was a village my mother hadn't set foot in for seven decades.

All things considered, then, how silly I'd been to think that I, whose family had been in America for many decades, would read life in the same way as my Bahraini students, who, for all their travels to Europe and access to the Internet, still lived in a tiny desert kingdom, as I was reminded each time the air became unusually opaque and sand storms blew in from the west. Or I could just look around me. On the littered streets of the *souk*, along the boulevard that edged the sea, in the hotel lobby with its enormous chandeliers and sweeping staircases, women like dark shadows. Swathed in black from head to foot, sometimes only their eyes showing, sometimes not. Even a century and more ago, in the hills of Lebanon, my grandmother had never dressed like that.

No, this wasn't Lebanon, to which Western missionaries, educators, tourists, bankers, and artists had been coming since at least the 19th century. Flourishing there, establishing businesses, churches, hospitals, and universities. And for a millennium before that, a series of more militant invaders from Byzantium, Rome, and this same Arabian peninsula, and then Crusaders. Again, my students had gotten it right: "Lebanese are different," they'd said. "They have different ideas." After reading a chapter on late-19th-century emigration to America, one student wrote, "What most surprises me is the courage of Lebanese women to go into a new land . . . especially those who went there by themselves. . . . Nowadays [in Bahrain], women have to take permission from their husbands to go out and it's a taboo if the woman asked to spend the night over in another house, even if it was her brother's." His wonder was enough to raise a blush of pride as long as I let myself forget that, after 15 years of civil war and another 15 of uncertain recuperation, Beirut remains a synonym for savagery and sectarian hate.

Now, if Lebanese seemed so alien to my students, how much more so Lebanese-Americans. And here I'd been, imagining I was practically one of them. I see now that I'd elided differences between us (just as we'd all disregarded what didn't suit us in the texts we read). I did it out of vanity and a desire to belong. With such false assumption bundled into my luggage, it was inevitable that I would occasionally be humbled or confused.

All term as my students struggled to read the literature of the course, I struggled to read them. More than once, I'd head back to my hotel after class and tell my American colleague, "Their responses are so strange." But with each new text I got a new lease on life. They'd shown little sympathy for Hamod—those who spoke up—but surely their hearts would go out to little Nadia and her brother Mikhi. And so they did, but only up to a point. Which is to say that the children's abusive uncle came out looking relatively good. Barbara's plight, I decided, would hit closer to home; we would be of one mind when it came to her impossible mother. "That sweet woman," one student said. Finally I thought I had them deciphered. That's when a group of them pulled the rug out from under me by falling for Saroya.

When I sat down with their essays, it was like reading an amended text. Some voices that had been mostly quiet in class were now joining in and taking issue. Some voices that had been heard all along were now making more nuanced statements, articulating more complicated thoughts. Everyone reaching more strenuously for understanding. When my students at home would ask me what I was looking for in their writing, I'd say, "Above all, to see your mind at work." In the essays of my Bahraini students, I found what I was always hoping for. And also generosity of spirit.

In Bahrain, I'd been expecting a mirror and found a window. It just took a while for me to know the difference. And finally to be glad that in looking at my students, I wasn't merely staring at my own face. Though, yes, I could still detect a family resemblance.

Evelyn with her students in Damascus

A Fullbright in Damascus

NEIGHBORHOOD

I loved the sound of it, loved to give it out as my address. Shari' Nuri Basha, the street (*shari'*) on which I lived for four months. Long enough to feel at home. A plaque at one end identified the honorable Basha as the Turkish governor of Damascus in the last years of the Ottoman era. Even when the empire fell and the French moved in, the street name held.

Except that there is more to the story. Sometime in the 1940s, Syrian officials re-named the narrow lane in honor of the British emissary Sir Edward Spears, a latter-day Lawrence of Arabia, who had argued strenuously for Syrian independence. The tribute was short lived. Within a decade, maybe two, Shari' Spears was no more, Nuri Basha had reclaimed his ancient place. My guess is there came a moment, after Suez or leading up to it, when Damascenes were in no mood to think kindly of any Englishman.

It was not a long street, my Nuri Basha. I could walk it in under 10 minutes, from the busy commercial intersection, known as Jisr el-Abyad (the White Bridge), up to the far end that stopped just short of the American Language school and, below that "the Tent of the Nation," a popular site of rallies against America's Middle East policies. At either end of the street, not on Nuri Basha itself but set close to it, was a mosque. The one at Jisr el-Abyad was the landmark I looked for when watching from the microbus for my stop, the taller, prettier one I called "my" mosque because I passed it so often as I went about my day and was caught up more than once in the stream of worshippers converging on it at noon or before dusk.

Summoned by the muezzin, they hurried from every direction, sober-faced men and boys. One faith, one purpose. Though a woman and a non-believer, I was comforted by their company as they caught up with me and passed me, but I was also wistful. No comparable community to embrace me, I mused; no comparable rituals to sustain me. During Ramadan, when the mosque could not hold all the worshippers, the last to arrive lined up in the yard: tiers of men, now standing erect, now bowing toward Mecca, now kneeling with foreheads and palms to the ground. I slowed my pace as I passed, but I knew enough not to pull out my camera. On the sidewalk, an old man sat cross-legged on a kitchen chair he'd set under a tree. He was polishing shoes the men had slipped off at the gate, lining them up neatly on a stone wall when he was done. It had the feel of piety. Though it was business, of course, and location was everything.

From mosque to mosque, the *shari'*, lined with apartment buildings, ran through a middle-class neighborhood, which was respectable certainly but not chic as it had been in General Spears's day. Since then, Ottoman homes with courtyards and fountains had been razed, aristocrats had moved on, workaday shops had lodged themselves in every available cranny.

I remember greengrocers, most of whose produce—whether lemons or marrow squash, onions or apples—went for one price; my purchases were heaped on a scale, and I paid by weight for the lot. I remember a pharmacy, where an avuncular druggist prescribed a

blend of jasmine and thyme tea for my cold and taught me to interpret the Celsius thermometer he'd just sold me. "Here"—he pointed
with the tip of his pencil—"you must call the doctor." I remember a
stationer's, where a sweet-faced young woman sold me index cards
for my Arabic class. My last week in Damascus, already nostalgic for
what I was leaving behind, I asked to take her picture. She smiled.
"My husband would not like it." "Don't tell him," I said. "It's just to
remember you by." She smiled again: "Not tell my husband? That is
impossible."

I remember too a beauty salon that I never saw anyone enter or
leave; a computer place, where I picked up floppy discs; a dusty
antique shop with brass trays on display in the window; and two
bakeries—one so diffident it took me weeks to notice it and then
only because someone pointed it out. I remember the shop where I
bought minutes for my cell phone; on my second visit, the clerk asked
me, "news aside," did I like Damascus. It took a minute to catch on
that he meant, "discounting politics." In that same block, a lone up-
holsterer labored over his work, early and late, sometimes even on
Friday, the day of rest, never once (that I saw) glancing up or out toward the street and its light. Nearby, the French school, a remnant of
the street's glory days, occupied a stone building with a handsome
facade; children hung out on the massive steps, exotic in their dark
blue uniforms, bright bandannas, and pink or tan backpacks. Closer
to Jisr el-Abyad, a dentist's office, down half a flight from the street,
seemed to do most of its business after dark. Behind its bare windows,
a mime show played out in the lamplight—a patient supine in the
chair, gripping its arms, while the dentist stooped over him, doing
unpleasant things in his mouth. Outside, a rust-colored shingle
displayed a single large tooth.

"Look for the tooth," I told my would-be visitors. It was on the
top floor of that building that I had my flat. Nominally, the fourth
floor, though with the high ceilings of the apartments below and

steep staircases, it felt more like the sixth. But the light and the views justified everything. Not part of the original building, my rooms had been added on as a kind of penthouse. Its broad expanse of balcony, washed by morning sunshine, was good for drying the laundry I draped over outdoor chairs. Across the rooftops, I saw the downtown skyline, smudged with pollution. Over the railing, I looked down at Nuri Basha, parked up on both sides with Nissans and such resting their haunches on the sidewalks. Down the middle, one-way traffic pushed through.

But it was the smaller balcony, to the rear and off the kitchen, that had sold me on the place. It hung above a terraced courtyard planted with persimmon, magnolia, loquat, and lemon trees and with climbing vines that blossomed white even in September. Between the trees, bamboo canopies had been erected by conservative newcomers. If they could help it, no decent man would ogle their women from an upper story. Of course, what was screened off was also screened in. Though the women could hear gulls screech overhead, they could not watch them reel through the air or notice the curious few touch down on rooftops, think better of it, and soar off again. Beyond their careening, the landscape rose steeply, building at length into a mountain.

Legend has it that Mohammed, catching his first glimpse of lush Damascus from that height, refused to pass down into the city since man is allowed to enter but once into paradise. These days, with Damascus swimming in smog, the spectacular view is in the opposite direction. I took it in at night from my balcony or, when the weather turned cold, from behind my kitchen windows. The mountain festooned with lights—starry clusters of houses, strings of headlights and, on a steep ridge, the neon glow of restaurants that seemed placed there on a dare. Tucked in on one slope and on another, mosques stood watch, their minarets bathed in green light, vantage points where I liked to imagine the Prophet might have paused.

I slept well and woke early.

Breakfast was always the same, concocted from old habit and Syrian custom. Yogurt into which I stirred sliced banana, grapes, fresh mint, and almonds; dried thyme moistened with olive oil, scooped up in paper-thin bread; green olives and Turkish coffee that I sipped from a demitasse while watching the BBC news. Occasionally, a soft-boiled egg.

To put that rather simple meal together meant visits to five merchants in the neighborhood. Not that there weren't one-stop American-style supermarkets in Damascus, but I never felt the urge to track one down. It would have been like signing a lease on the expensive apartment a realtor showed me when I first arrived. It was up-to-date, he argued, and convenient to the university where I'd be teaching. But why, I wondered, did he think I would travel all the way to Damascus—Damascus, of all places—to live in a high-rise on a highway. Likewise, why pass up the personal transactions on Nuri Basha, where customers greeted shopkeepers with, "God give you strength"? And shopkeepers called after their customers, "Go in peace."

Around the corner from Nuri Basha, I had my nut man, whom I twice discovered with his head on the counter, stealing a catnap; after school his grandson helped out. One day the boy emerged from the back room, a glass of water in his hand. He held it out to me, he said he'd heard me cough. Across from the nut shop, I had my coffee man, who recommended a grind laced with cardamom and, though clearly dismayed by my ignorance, explained how to brew it. I kept wanting to say (if my Arabic had been more agile), "I really do know, I'm just double-checking." Yogurt and eggs came from a store a few steps from my building, so tiny that only three customers could crowd in at once; if the owner came out from behind his counter, one of the three would have to retreat. The yogurt, made fresh each day, he sold in a little pail. I'd skim off the wrinkled skin to get at the silky *laban* underneath, good as what my mother produced when I was a child.

Olives and bread (also cheese, chocolate bars, and cleaning supplies) I picked up at a larger establishment down the street. There, as in other shops, a division of labor prevailed. A middle-aged man sat at the cash register while his son waited on customers. The father totted up the bill, took my money, and gave back my change. But, like most Syrian merchants, he didn't expect to be paid to the penny. If my bill came to 105 lira, he'd take 100 and wave off the extra coin. His gesture spoke clearly: "We are not money grubbers." For his part, the son was so affable that I was encouraged to try out my Arabic. When he assembled my purchases on the counter, I'd say, *Salam dayaatuk*, "Bless your hands." "Bless *you*," he'd politely reply. When he had a bad cold, I murmured *Salaamtuk*, I wish you health, remembering an old woman who'd once said it to me while making the sign of the cross over my head.

For fruits (or vegetables), I had several options. One was the grocery behind the mosque at Jisr el-Abyad. The first time I dropped by, the proprietor fingered his wedding band and pointed to me—he was asking if I was married. After that, I shopped there only as a last resort. A grocery at the opposite end of Nuri Basha was a bit of a walk if I had much to carry, but the produce was fresh and it was varied. And then there was the street vendor on the corner, who sold fruits and vegetables out of his truck and out of the crates he unloaded each morning onto the sidewalk. His prices, like those of the grocery stores, were ridiculously low. My first week in Damascus, I noted in my journal that I'd spent a total of 40 cents on Swiss chard, onions, a huge bunch of mint, and two cucumbers. This man got most of my business. Partly because he was nearest, and partly because he literally had no roof over his head. "All winter?" I asked him. "You are here?" He nodded yes.

On the opposite corner, another street vendor stationed himself each day, a man with a weathered face and missing teeth who might well have been younger than he looked. But when I asked him his name, he replied, as an old man would—*abu Khaled*, "father of

Khaled." He had one of those carts on wheels, with an umbrella, that Americans buy hot dogs from at the beach, except his held hot fava beans (in Arabic *fuul*). When a customer showed, he ran through a simple routine: ladle beans out of simmering water, slip into a plastic baggie, add salt and cumin, and shake. That was his work, achingly boring. But he did it with care (as if for Khaled) and he smiled at his patrons. It worried me that he didn't seem to have many, except when the French school let out and children swarmed down the street, though the beans were delicious and, again, impossibly cheap, the equivalent of 20 cents a bag. A coin at a time, how could he manage? I asked for double servings.

Nuri Basha was where I started and ended the day. But beyond it were a slew of destinations I might make my way to. That most were still within walking distance expanded my sense of ownership; whatever I could get to on foot was, by definition, in my general neighborhood. For instance, the restaurants in Restaurant Square when I wasn't up to cooking, the lounge of the Cham Palace Hotel where my cousin stayed when she visited from the Gulf, the travel agency across from the Four Seasons that arranged my Christmas trip to Aleppo and Krak de Chevalier, the government immigration office that in better days would easily have given me permission to cross to Lebanon and back, the British Airways office where (for $200) I postponed my date of departure for the States; the crafts market—housed in what had been an Ottoman school—where I shopped for a backgammon board inlaid with rosewood, olive wood, and mother of pearl.

Across from the crafts market was the splendid national museum, its courtyard teeming with a surplus of treasures. On my first visit, I wove my way among outcroppings of ancient pediments and around Corinthian capitals that sprouted left and right like mushrooms. A blaze of color against an outdoor wall turned out to be a mosaic of a griffin sinking its fangs into a bull while a bear tore at the rump of an antelope, and a frantic ostrich tried to shake a leopard off its back. In front of the mosaic a no-nonsense lion, carved from basalt, held his ground. Inside the museum and down some stairs, I came upon a burial chamber from the Valley of the Tombs in Palmyra (Queen Zenobia's desert city) and rare frescoes from a third-century synagogue, which—after nearly two millennia buried in the sand—had been excavated near the border with Iraq. Outside again, I circled a pair of stylized herons installed in a pool, one intently grooming itself, the other, its neck stretched tall, its beak open in a squawk. From the world of the ancients, they ushered me back to the contemporary.

Closer, again, to Nuri Basha were the "Friday" *souk* that catered to locals and sold more dishpans than beaded lamps and inlaid boxes; the French patisserie where I got my fix of cappuccino; the stylist who wanted to frost my hair (*Laysh la'*—"Why not?"—I heard myself say); the tailor who replaced a zipper in my jacket for $1.50; the shops on and off Shari' Hamra where I found a cell phone, a tea kettle, a vegetable scraper, and a tape recorder, and came that close to buying a yoga mat; the florist on the broad avenue called Abu Rumana (Father of Pomegranates), the confectionary shop close by that had won an international prize for its dipped chocolates. Uphill from the chocolates, the American embassy and the American Cultural Center—as a Fulbright Fellow, I had access to both. I relied on them for my Internet connections, the easy exchange of travelers' checks for lira, the cafeteria that served a hot meal for a couple of bucks.

AMERICANS, GOOD SAMARITANS, AND CABBIES

They were also where I ran into other Americans, a dozen or so, on grants from the State Department. It took me by surprise. After all, President Bush had as much as accused Syria of assassinating Rafic Hariri, the former Lebanese prime minister, and, to drive home the point, had withdrawn our ambassador. I puzzled over the politics. Puzzled even more over why Americans were competing to come. I, at least, had family roots in the area, but most of the others did not. Why weren't they scared off by what they'd heard from politicians or read in the papers?

The answer most gave was straightforward. For the sake of their studies or their careers, they needed to work on their Arabic, and Syria was the best place for that. "Not Lebanon?" I asked, putting in a word for my parents' homeland. Oh, no, I was told, the Lebanese speak only English and French. Syria also appealed as a tourist's paradise—Roman ruins, "dead" Byzantine cities, a Crusader castle, Biblical settings. Damascus—even the name was magic—once the center of the Muslim caliphate and said by many to be the oldest continuously inhabited city in the world. But mostly, I think, it was their own nature that had lured these Americans. Curious, eager to venture beyond the familiar, many—even the young—had already lived overseas. If there was a popular bias against a particular country, they were the sort who would ask "Why?" Who might even think, "Makes it more interesting."

Of the Americans I got to know—those who weren't just faces or names to me—a few lived nearby. As with the shops, I loved that easy proximity. Roland, for instance, was a Fulbright student whose flat lay just east of the Italian hospital, near a bakery with a gaping oven where I sometimes bought meat pies. Roland's goal was a career in the Foreign Service, and, though only 22, he was well on his way. He'd grown up speaking French at home, was proficient in Spanish, and had served student internships at the Pentagon and at the American embassies in Nicaragua and Argentina. But it was the Middle East that he had his eye on. That's why he'd come to Syria, to build on the one year of Arabic he'd had in the States and to find out if he'd be happy in the region. The answer was *yes*—"I knew that from the first week," he told me. "I could see myself here for a long time."

He had another reason as well. It was the political ferment. "I like being where things are happening," he said, "things people pay attention to." What might put somebody else off, I could see, was exactly what appealed to him. During my first weeks in Damascus, a massive political protest was held at the Plaza of the Seven Seas. With feeling running high against the United States, the embassy had advised us to steer clear, but Roland went to have a look. "Did you run into any trouble?" I asked him. We were having a lunch of *mezza* and fried eggs in my apartment. "No," he said. In fact, firemen had helped him climb onto their truck to get a better view. It was because of his camera; like demonstrators everywhere, they wanted the world to see. And yet, one week earlier, when he had been taking innocuous pictures of mountain and mosque, a member of the secret police had come "out of nowhere," temporarily confiscated his digital camera and gone through its memory card.

The route to Tarey's apartment zigzagged downhill, passing not far from the empty residence of the American ambassador, guarded still by a contingent of Syrians in uniform. Tarey was something of an old hand in the region. She'd taught for two years in Jordan and for five in Kuwait and been married for 13 years to a Palestinian from whom she was now divorced. Eventually, she landed a job at the University of Michigan. But Tarey was happiest overseas. "Every time I go back to the States," she told me, "I feel chains wrap around my wrists."

"Why Syria?" I asked her over coffee at the posh Cham Hotel. Hadn't she been put off by its dark reputation? No, she said; back home she'd had Syrian friends, their country didn't seem so alien, she'd jumped at the chance to come. And Syria had not disappointed: She liked the easy pace, she liked the people, and she realized that, professionally, she had finally come into her own. In that sense, Syria was, she said, "a life-changing experience." At Michigan, she had felt used and invisible, working hard yet not respected by senior faculty;

in Syria she had authority and autonomy, running workshops for teachers of English in every pocket of the country. So when Michigan warned her that her academic leave was up, she knew she couldn't go back. Just like that, she gave up the security of a position at a major American university, and did it, she told me, "without even blinking an eye."

Recently Tarey had been coordinating her travels with Mary, an American colleague who had an identical government grant and had also taught overseas: two years in Iran, another two in Australia, one year in Portugal, eight months in Indonesia, and a shorter stint in China. (What, I brooded, had I been doing with my life?) But, unlike Tarey and Roland, Mary had to be coaxed to Damascus. Was it safe? Would she be lonely? Syria didn't sound like a place where a woman would be comfortable on her own. We chatted about it one afternoon, sitting on her balcony, which offered an even more stunning view than mine of Mount Kassium. I'd reached her place by walking along the Barada River; once it had watered the Damascus oasis but now, in this season, it was a disheartening sight, a bed of mud and rocks littered with trash.

Despite her misgivings, Mary had decided that this grant opportunity was "too good to miss," and within a month of her arrival she knew she'd chosen well. The teaching was wonderful, and the Syrian people had won her heart. She loved walking into a shop and being treated "as if it's almost an honor you're there." She loved it that if she stood on a sidewalk with a guidebook in her hand, "within about 15 seconds, someone comes up to ask, in English, *Can I help you?*" I was reminded of a story Roland had told me about his first day in Syria, when he'd been lost. People on the street had taken the trouble to help him out, actually lugging his bags to his hotel.

When it came to helpfulness, I had corroborating evidence of my own, starting with strangers I approached for directions, who often walked me halfway to my destination. Once a butcher who didn't have the lamb I'd set my heart on, advised me to try a second shop. Not far away, he said, and tried to explain. I must have looked uncertain. "Wait," he said, and appealed to another customer. "Please, my brother—may God lengthen your days—go with her." The man said, "Come," and led the way. When I asked my nut man where to find the best cheese pies, he pointed across the street. But, worried that I might not be able to negotiate my purchase, he put a battered wooden chair in his doorway and motioned me to follow. At the bakery, he explained to the workers what I wanted and drew my attention to other good things they had on display. Then hurried back to take in his chair, open again for business.

The Good Samaritan I remember best is the young man who helped me make it home one evening from the university. By the time my class let out, it was dark; taxis whizzed by and wouldn't stop. In a fit of impatience, I decided to walk. "It can't be that far," I thought. Ahead of me, I saw a woman striding along and decided to follow—surely she was heading back to the city center. From there, I could find my way. Her purposefulness inspired confidence, which gave way to doubt when she swerved off in what had to be the wrong direction. The street she'd led me to was deserted, except for a young couple on a park bench. I was hesitant about intruding, but I was also lost. When I explained where I lived, the young man shook his head. "You cannot walk." Leaving the girlfriend on her own, he took me to the nearest busy thoroughfare, consulted with an older couple standing on the curb, then hailed a microbus, checked with the driver, and invited me to get on. I was in luck, the bus would let me off a few steps from home.

On board, I fell into conversation with a teenage boy who got off with me at my stop and stayed with me until he was sure I had my bearings. Then he shook my hand and went on his way. Earlier a Syrian woman had advised me not to ride the buses—she never did. But I found them friendly places, where other passengers were always eager to alert me to my stop and, on two occasions, quietly paid my fare before I was aware.

And Mary herself also helped me. In one sitting, she charted my neighborhood for me, marking up a city map with arrows and X's—here's your apartment, here's mine, here's Tarey's, here's a good hair dresser, here's where you go for a flu shot, here's the British library that lends books, here's my butcher. On the phone one day, I told her I wasn't feeling so well. "If you're worse in the middle of the night," she said, "call me. I'll take you to the hospital." Later, when I thanked her, she explained, "That's what we have to do for each other, because we're women and we're alone." But beyond the claims of sisterhood, she was learning from the Syrians that it was important to say to people, "I will be there for you," and equally important to be able to say, "I need you now." When her Syrian friends found out that she'd been having panic attacks, they asked, "Why are you suffering and being afraid by yourself? What is the point of that?" Good question, she thought. What was this fetish about being independent?

On her patio that day, Mary told me another story, how she'd been walking down the street and passed under a balcony just as someone carelessly spilled a pan of water over the railing. When she let out a yelp, the whole street froze, and then people rushed over to see what was wrong. More reason, as she said, to "feel perfectly safe here." I knew what she meant. Cautious when I first arrived, I soon had no qualms about walking home alone, even at midnight. The virtues of a police state, I theorized.

But crossing a busy street—now *that* was dangerous. In Beirut, the traffic had also been horrendous—narrow streets, few traffic lights, too many cars jostling for position. But I'd soon learned that, if I stepped off the curb, drivers would pull up short. In Damascus, on the other hand, a pedestrian testing the traffic was seen as fair game. With time, I learned when to make a dash for it, but I had to stay alert.

Taxis were especially aggressive. Once, my cab cut off another—
not unusual but it was done in an egregious manner. The other driver
wasn't going to take it. He kept pulling in front of us and slamming
on his brakes. I noticed a motorist beside us gesturing to my driver,
as if gently tamping something down, miming the message "Keep
calm." I thought the ugliness was over, I wanted to be on my way.
That's when the other cabbie leapt out of his car and rushed at us,
pulling my driver out from behind the wheel and wrestling him to
the ground while I sat in the back seat, stunned and helpless. But just
as strangers rushed to the rescue when Mary screeched, so a small
crowd hurried over to pull the brawlers apart and, like that other
nameless motorist, to urge patience. It was a specimen of community
in action. At home, I thought, no one would want to get involved.

Truth to tell, Syrian taxi drivers were the bane of my existence. "The
enemy," I'd grumble and then feel ashamed. These were poor men, I
reminded myself, who worked long hours driving rattletrap cars on
streets that were like battlefields. And, if they did overcharge me, what
did it come to? An extra 50 cents or, at most, a dollar? Still, something
in me was determined not to be outsmarted. For instance, cabs were
supposed to be equipped with meters. If I didn't see one, I learned to
ask at the outset about the fare. One day I jumped out of three taxis in
succession when the drivers wanted to charge me two or three times
what I knew was fair. If the cab had a meter, I'd make a point of asking
that it be turned on. One driver started it running, all right, but set it
ahead, thinking I wouldn't notice. Before I was familiar with the streets,
drivers might take me all around the barn—"too much traffic," they'd
say, dismissing the more direct route in case I had an inkling. It was
hard to win. But there were comic moments: the driver who told me
he couldn't run the meter during Ramadan, the one who charged me
"for benzene," the jolly one who met me halfway on the fare and then
serenaded me to my destination. "Don't worry, be happy," he sang,
showing off his baritone, his good will, and his English.

The problem was, I couldn't do without cabs. They were the only convenient transportation to the university and back, as well as the quickest way to the endless attractions of the Old City—its sprawling bazaar, its magnificent mosque (said to hold the head of John the Baptist), its Ottoman palace, its maze of cobblestone lanes (some so narrow that autos can snake through only with side-view mirrors retracted), its balconies that almost meet overhead (so close that neighbors can shake hands across the street or pass a plate of *baqlawa*), the house—the very window—from which St. Paul was lowered in a basket (or so it is claimed), the ancient Roman arch and old city gates, the new boutique hotels, the myriad shops that sell craftwork and antiques (some authentic, some not).

I made it to the Old City several times a week, always by cab, though I finally learned to catch a microbus home. Aside from its general attractions, the Old City was home to my Arabic tutor and to a Syrian family who had kindly taken me in soon after I arrived. Also to another Fulbright student who had been the first American to befriend me. When I'd wondered how to get my luggage up all those stairs to my flat, Jim had volunteered to help; he and a friend would do it. Earlier he'd walked me to have a look at a vacant apartment he'd ferreted out. (It wasn't right for me, but I was grateful.) He'd taken me to my first restaurant in the Old City, housed in a restored Ottoman home—the kind of place where, if you ask, they bring you backgammon with your coffee. We sat above the tiled courtyard, snacking on fresh vegetables and on hummus garnished with savory ground lamb. Listening to the gurgle of the fountain.

Like Roland, Jim was in Syria to improve his Arabic, though he seemed fluent to me. Of course, he'd had a head start: four years as an Arabic Studies major at Brigham Young University, and a chunk of that time—four months—living and studying right here in Damascus. After returning home and graduating, he'd taken a job as a translator for a firm that served doctors' offices and hospitals. Jim worked with Spanish-speaking patients (as a young Mormon missionary, he'd spent two years in Argentina) and those whose first language was Arabic. This time around in Damascus, he would be auditing courses in the faculty of medicine in order to expand his medical vocabulary.

It didn't take long to realize that Jim was of a serious turn of mind, the large decisions and small details of his life governed by his faith. Yet he felt a degree of affinity with Muslims. When he heard them speak out against abortion, his reaction was "Go, Islam!" But first and last it was the Arabic language that beguiled him, the way the name of God infused even casual conversation. Ask a man how he is, Jim said, and he'll say, "Thanks be to God." In other words, he's fine.

Through Jim, I met an older American couple, also members of the Church of Jesus Christ of Latter Day Saints. They lived nearby, in a high-ceilinged apartment around the corner from one embassy, across from another, and down the street from a fenced in park where a vendor sold plastic toys and pink cotton candy.

I'd known that young Mormons usually devote a couple of years to missionary work, but it was news to me that retirees often do the same. In Syria, the aim was not to proselytize, which the government forbade, but to offer technical expertise. Larry had been a professor of agricultural science at Brigham Young University. Now he was working with the faculty of agriculture at Damascus University, editing their scientific abstracts, calling their attention to new statistical models, tutoring them in English, making suggestions. Through his efforts and those of BYU colleagues who had preceded him, the department had expanded its library and acquired a cannery, a weather station, an egg hatcher, and—from America—bull semen. (Ingenuity won the day against U.S. restrictions on trade.) His wife, Raili, also spent her days on campus, teaching English.

I was impressed. Larry and Raili had left behind their seven children and umpteen grandchildren to live for two years in a land about which they knew nothing and whose language they could not speak or understand. And had done so at their own expense. "If you're paying for it," Raili explained, "that means you really want to do it." Certainly, they were working harder than I could imagine myself doing—leaving the house at 7:30 in the morning, returning at 3:00 and teaching students at home, sometimes until nine o'clock at night. "It's therapy," Raili said, "because we'd sure get homesick if we didn't have much to do."

To Raili (and, no doubt, to Larry) as to Jim, certain Muslim values rang true—chastity, generosity, family solidarity—as did certain rituals. During Ramadan, she fasted as she used to one day a month at home. She'd also learned from the Syrians. Sounding very much like Mary, she said, "I've never been a friend like they are." There were the two young schoolteachers, for instance, who couldn't bear the thought of her and Larry being on their own so far from home. "Look," they said, "you don't have your children here. We will do anything for you. We will take you anywhere. We will come and clean your house. We will treat you like our parents."

One night I found myself at dinner with another American couple, also older, who were attached to a local NGO. Over dinner, the wife— I'll call her Ellen—did most of the talking. I soon saw she was full of good works, buying Christmas toys for orphans, changing bed linens at a hospital for lepers, looking into the exploitation of Filipino domestics. I saw too that she was a person of decided opinions about Syrians, whom she referred to as *these people*. In fact, though she and her husband had been in the country only a few months, she was already threatening to write a book cataloguing their faults, which in her eyes ranged from rudeness to fanaticism. One man had actually told her—I took her at her word—that he'd be happy to blow himself up for a political cause. "But do you think that's typical?" I asked her. "Oh, yes," she said.

And then there was the business about her father. Not long after they'd arrived in Syria, word had come that he was dying. Ellen and her husband made a brief visit home to say good-bye. Syrian acquaintances were surprised that she hadn't stayed longer, to see her father through to his end. But her husband had had to return, she told me, and her place was with him; in their decades of marriage, they'd been apart for perhaps a total of two weeks. "*These people*," she said, "don't love the way we do."

I would think of Ellen weeks later, on a tour of sights outside Damascus. My driver, Fawaz, was reporting how he'd tried and failed to get a visa to visit his brother in the States. After putting him off several times, an officer at the embassy had come out with the truth. The fear was that, once in America, Fawaz would deliberately melt into the landscape and never return. This was a man with a good job, who owned his own house, was married, and had three daughters. As he spoke, he shook his head in bewilderment. "Don't Americans love their children?" he asked me. "If I am away from my girls for five days, I am like this"—he pantomimed wiping away tears.

A TRIO OF FREELANCERS

Among Ellen's other pronouncements—"American women who marry Syrians can *never* break into the closed circle of the family." A statement belied by at least one American woman I met, the daughter of an activist Protestant minister. After her marriage to a Syrian Muslim, Deborah moved into the home he shared with his mother, his aunt, a brother and his wife, and their children. Nine people in a house with only three bedrooms. But she called that household a blessing that had taught her the satisfaction of connectedness and also the beauty of hierarchy, with a matriarch—her mother-in-law—perched at the top. "We had a terrific relationship," Deborah told me. For instance, as soon as the older woman understood that her son and Deborah had decided not to have children, she defended that choice against family members who raised nosy questions. "She was like a lioness," Deborah said. "She would just put them in their place and there was no more talking about it."

Deborah belonged to a category of Westerners—most of the ones I happened to meet were women—who had come to Syria without benefit of government subsidy or sponsorship. For that reason, they seemed to me the most adventurous of all. Would I ever have thrown caution to the wind as they had? For Deborah, it was the first Gulf War that had turned her face eastward; it stirred "a deep desire to understand the Middle East." And so, even as fighting raged, she signed a contract to teach music at a school in Damascus. "You know the word *naseeb*?" Deborah asked me. "It means destiny—something that is designed for you and you will meet it one way or another because it's yours."

But it seemed to me that Deborah made her own *naseeb*; she knew her mind and followed her instincts. When she announced she was off to Damascus, the response from family and friends was not encouraging, except for her mother's wary congratulations. "Of my three daughters," she said, "I understand you the least, but, as I watch you in your life, you make decisions—I have no idea how you got there, why you got there, but I see you continually land on your feet. So you must know what you're doing." In Damascus one evening, soon after she'd arrived, Deborah turned down an invitation to an "American" event—obeying her impulse to avoid compatriots—and attended instead a "Syrian" gathering. That night she met her husband.

These days Deborah is as much at home in Syria as in the United States, moving between the two, teaching yoga and piano as easily in one place as the other. In an arrangement many would envy, she and her husband spend half the year in Damascus (now that his mother is gone, they have their own apartment in the old city) and half in Vermont, where they have set up a weaving workshop on their property and sell Syrian rugs out of their home. Potential customers hear about their wares by word of mouth, come to shop, and stay to visit. "We serve Arabic coffee and apricots or dates," Deborah told me, "and we tell stories, allowing Arab culture just to unfold."

"I would not recommend anybody do what I did," Theresa said. "I was taking a tremendous risk." It's a late afternoon in November. She's arrived home from the [International] American Language School, where she teaches, and we are sitting in the dining room of the apartment that was once her in-laws' and to which she came as a bride. Over the years, father-in-law, then her husband, then her mother-in-law have died; her children have married and moved away. Now Theresa lives alone except for an old family retainer, a gentleman who picks up warm bread from the bakery each day, shops for groceries, does light ironing, and, when the fruit is in season, cooks up apricot jam. As we nibble on croissants and drink tea he's brewed, she tells me her story.

Some 40 years ago, in Geneva, Theresa met the man of her dreams. He was a Syrian graduate student at the university there; she was a young Englishwoman working for the World Health Organization. One day, well into their relationship, he announced that, degree in hand, he would soon head back to Syria. "What about us?" she asked. "You couldn't live in Damascus," was the reply. But she was determined, and, though they were separated for the next two years (due to the Six-Day War and its aftermath), they married. "Today," she told me, "I know there's more than one fish in the ocean. But I was just so much in love. This was the person I wanted. I think it was growing up in the fifties, on a diet of Hollywood movies and romantic fantasy."

From the beginning, the reality wasn't easy. She'd been raised as a Roman Catholic; his family were Eastern Orthodox Christians. To her distress, he insisted that they wed in his church. "What difference does it make to you?" she said. "You don't go to church." But, though she calls him "one of the most considerate people I've ever known," on this point he was adamant. A matter of male pride, she later speculated, the fear of seeming to kowtow to his bride. After the wedding, they moved in with his parents, and (unlike Deborah) she chafed at that arrangement. For one thing, nothing in her small-town background had prepared her for the busy social life his family led.

Visitors had been used to dropping by all the time. Now there was the added incentive of congratulating the groom and his family and meeting the bride. Her role was to hand around juice, cookies, coffee, chocolates—in that order. She could barely understand a word of Arabic. Each visit had to be repaid—another two hours "sitting on an uncomfortable sofa, not knowing what was going on." When people made the effort to speak French (in which Theresa was fluent), her mother-in-law still dominated the conversation. "She was extremely intelligent," Theresa says, "had a strong personality, years of wisdom, lots of social skills, and was very interested in politics. She could sit in a roomful of men and hold her own." Watching her in action, Theresa felt inadequate or as if she had no personality of her own.

And she was lonely. No close friends at first, and a husband whose own friends, family, and colleagues made significant demands on his time. She did have a full-time job teaching English. "That was my lifeline," she says. But, other than going to work or visiting other families, she was encouraged to stick close to home: "My husband and his parents were so protective." Once, when she wandered off, just to have something to do, a family friend was astonished to find her walking by herself. He escorted her back to the family apartment.

In the long run, her marriage was "happy and successful." But it was just luck, she says, that she landed in a family with whom— despite differences in habit—she got on. "You talk to other Westerners here, and you can hear such terrible horror stories about interference from parents." In fact, her new family turned out to be a lot of fun. Not just her husband, who was given to practical jokes, but also the older generation, wonderful raconteurs who—once she learned Arabic—could keep her entertained for hours. Especially, as it turned out, the country cousins, with their hilarious stories of racing across town, from one kiosk to another, looking for bread; motoring miles into the hills to buy cooking gas; or smuggling toilet paper in from Lebanon. There was a lesson there, the way her husband's people transmuted privation into comedy. Another lesson learned, Theresa says, was tolerance: the forbearance exercised by Syrians toward foreigners, people of other religions, and—most challenging of all—difficult older relatives. The kindness with which Syrians treat the elderly, she says, "should be an example to Westerners."

Her final verdict: "At the end of it all, I'm a better person. I know part of it comes with age and experience. But, if I had never left England, I fear I would be like so many insular Brits who, even today, think they're so superior to everybody else and look down on people in the third world or sometimes even people just across the channel."

Betsy, a young American, didn't need to be warned about the pitfalls of cross-cultural romance—she'd experienced them for herself. A decade before I met her, she'd taught for a year in Kuwait. "I was interested in the Middle East," she says, using the term loosely. "It was always in the news, and I didn't get it at all. Sometimes I think the only way I can ever get anything is to go." Once in Kuwait, she became involved with a man who "ended up marrying his cousin." It was an arranged marriage, she says, something he didn't want but didn't feel he could oppose his family on. Betsy had known from the start that this marriage was in the works, but still it stung.

The next few years, she spent back in the States. Then came the second Gulf War. "I was so shocked," she says, "that Americans could be talked into that invasion." She gave herself a talking-to: "At least do a little something rather than just sit around and bitch." Also, as she admits, she was again primed for adventure. But why Syria? I got the standard response: "a good place to work on Arabic." But it was also the lure of the exotic: "Syria sounded mysterious."

Her family was worried. Her brother pleaded, "Please, don't go."

Betsy arrived in Damascus, enrolled in an Arabic class, and within a few weeks landed a position teaching English as a Second Language. And then, once again, she met a man. He ran a small dry-cleaning shop, where she took her clothes, and she fell into the habit of asking him for help with her Arabic homework. When he eventually suggested they go to his house to study, she got scared. Just as she had one night, early on, in a movie theater when the lights went out and the screen went black. She'd thought, "Dark room, Arabs, maybe if they figure out I'm an American, they're going to pounce." It took a while to lose that hair-trigger anxiety. He asked her again, "Come to my house, my mother is there." (Already this was an improvement on her experience in Kuwait, where her boyfriend had kept her a secret from his family.)

Their relationship grew into a romance, but one that she told herself had no future. The gulf was too great in terms of education, culture, religion, money. He's "poor, poor, poor," she wailed. And where would they live? For her it had to be the States. He was an only son, responsible for his mother. How could he leave her? And even if he agreed to, what work could he find in America? If he couldn't support his wife, it would be a desperate blow to his pride. Still there was no denying the spark between them, the excitement she hadn't found with more appropriate matches.

Of all the American and European women I met in Syria, Betsy was the most open and, in that sense, the most disarming. "You can ask me anything personal," she said. "Go anywhere, I don't care." Later in the same conversation, she laughed at herself. "I am such a tell-all." Her great preoccupation, of course, was what the future held for her and her boyfriend. Half serious, she once said, "I need you to be a shrink." The only advice I dared offer was trite enough: "As long as you're in this relationship, even if it's not forever, enjoy it for what it is and know that you're enjoying it."

I might just as well have been lecturing myself. In looking over the journal of my first few weeks in Syria, I have been surprised at all my griping: hotel room the size of a closet, a fever coming on, getting lost on campus, being ripped off by a cabbie, failure to connect with people whose names I'd been given by friends back home. I'd even lost my precious English-Arabic dictionary. Then, out of the blue, a journal entry that begins, "This is one of the best experiences of my life."

POLITICS

Betsy and her Australian roommate lived in a "refugee camp," the term used for a Palestinian ghetto on the outskirts of the city. Too far from everything, Betsy thought. It took her 45 minutes to get to the center of Damascus. Better to be where I was, in the heart of things and able to walk almost anywhere I wanted to go. But apartments in neighborhoods like mine were becoming more expensive. "It's the Iraqis," Betsy said. She was likely right. Since the American invasion in 2003, an estimated million and a half refugees have crossed the border into Syria, the cost of foods and basic goods has risen by 30 percent, and rents have doubled or even tripled. (The direct cost to the Syrian government is said to be 2 billion dollars a year.)

Until recently, Syria has allowed the free flow of Iraqi refugees into its territory. And, in comparison to Lebanon, it does well by its 400,000 Palestinians, allowing them to own businesses and property and providing them with social services. My first month in Syria, I went out to the camps one evening—a student in my class had invited me to an open house held every week at the home of Mazen, a man of about 50 I would guess. The guests were Palestinian and Syrian men, together with men and women from far-flung places like the United States, England, Sweden, Australia, and New Zealand. Arab women, whether Syrian or Palestinian, Muslim or Christian, were noticeably absent. At one point a group of children, who turned out to be Mazen's nieces and nephews, came in to greet the guests. With impeccable manners, they circled the room, shaking hands and smiling shyly before retreating to the upper floors. At 10:00, the buffet was laid and, though I'd eaten before I came, I snacked again on chicken and rice with almonds, eggplant dip, and the Middle Eastern version of baklava.

The food was tasty, and the people milling around the table, chatting in the living room, hanging out in the kitchen, were friendly and took an interest—what was I doing in Damascus and how did I like it? Mazen played the good host, silently taking me by the hand for a couple of dances. When I left at 3:30 a.m., the drinking and dancing and getting acquainted were still going strong. An aroused young Arab had just gathered a woman up in his arms and carried her to a sofa. As she pulled him closer, I slipped out of the room.

I never went back to Mazen's. I was too old to party all night (probably always had been), and the smoke—not just from unfiltered cigarettes but from the water pipe that Mazen had nursed at all evening—had done a number on me. ("An *arghili* in the house?" My Arabic tutor was astonished. "Mother would not allow it.") I awoke the next morning with a fiery sore throat and a cough that hung on for three weeks. What stayed with me longer and stays with me yet is the political discussion that night. I can't forget the exuberant young Palestinian who clowned and danced as if his only goal in life was to spread cheer. But when someone mentioned Israel, he turned fierce. "I want war," he said. "I don't want peace with these killers." He cited the massacre of Palestinians in the refugee camps of Sabra and Shatila (facilitated by the Israeli army) and the young Palestinian boy shot dead by Israeli soldiers while cowering behind his father. He wanted every Jew out of Palestine, by which he meant Israel, too. "Let them go back to wherever they came from." He paused before adding, "My father calls me an extremist."

Later, Mazen turned up the TV and the room grew quiet, everyone's attention riveted on the breaking story. The UN report on the assassination of the former prime minister of Lebanon had just been released, and, as expected, it implicated Syria. Murmurs of disapproval, sneers of derision. A young man from New Zealand harangued me with the injustice of it all. Like many in the room, he was ready to believe that Israel had killed Hariri, just to make Syria look bad. I had no way of telling, I said. Annoyed, he shifted ground: what did it matter, he said. Hariri had been a thug.

The assassination was on everyone's mind. Demonstrations in solidarity with the government were held downtown and on college campuses; banners were strung, tents erected to house crudely drawn cartoons. One day, when no one was around, I stepped inside a small tent to get a closer look. Arabic script was beyond me, but some captions were in English, and, in any case, the drawings themselves leapfrogged language barriers. One showed a balance scale, one side empty, the other side weighed down with American dollars. "Justice," it said. Another drawing showed a dove—American—in battle gear; beside it, another dove—Syrian—an olive branch in its mouth and blood spurting from a wound in its side as if the artist were channeling the iconography of Christ on the cross.

"I never tell people I'm American," Mary confided, "because I don't want to deal with the political agenda." One day, something happened that reinforced her reticence. As she was trying to hail a taxi, a well-dressed woman walked by and said to her, in perfect English, "Death to Americans," then continued a few paces, turned and spat in her direction. Unlike Mary, I did own up to being American. The usual response was "Welcome, welcome," sometimes followed by "But tell Bush not to come." If anyone asked me what I thought about the Hariri affair, I resorted to the dodge I'd used at Mazen's. "How can I know?" But it was the truth—how *could* I know? Still, because I was American, people wanted to bring me around to their way of thinking. They told me of warm relations between Hariri and Syrian president Bashar Assad. They pointed out the second house Hariri kept in Damascus. I craned to see it from the back seat of my cab. They claimed that, during the Lebanese civil war, thousands of Syrian soldiers had died trying to stop the fighting. "For what?" my driver, Fawaz, said. "Only out of brotherly love." Then he added, "We are not assassins." And that seemed to me the gist of it, what all the debate came to in the end. The cabbies, the store keepers, the pharmacists, the engineers—they knew *they* would not do such a deed. It followed, then, that neither would their government.

There were exceptions, the occasional Syrian willing to concede that Assad or his kin might well have had a hand in Hariri's murder if only as pawns of outside powers. But those who held to this view lowered their voices and spoke obliquely. Bashar Assad may not rule with quite the iron fist his father Hafez did, but Syria is still a police state, and memories of past atrocities still cast a shadow. No Syrian I met ever so much as alluded to the massacre at Hama—not in my presence. But, of course, I knew about the brutal reprisal taken in 1982 against the guerilla fighters of the Muslim Brotherhood. Faced with what he considered a dire personal threat and an intolerable insurgency against the authority of his government, Hafez resorted to naked force, bombing Hama (which the Brotherhood had declared a "liberated" city), then sending in tanks and artillery. When it was over, at least 10,000 residents of the city—civilians and fighters; men, women, and children—had been killed. (Some estimates put the number at 30,000 or higher.) In addition, much of the old section of the city, with its Ottoman-era palaces and mosques, had been destroyed.

The closest I came to glimpsing this dark underside of Syrian society was in my conversation with Nadia, a young woman who makes her living as an English translator. Her father had belonged to a banned political party that, as early as the 1980s, openly called

Hafez al-Assad a dictator. Things came to a head when Nadia's father wrote an article critical of the regime; the government came after him, and he had to go into hiding. Nadia was 11 months old. From time to time, while underground, he would get word to his wife to meet him in this city or that. According to Nadia, her mother never knew in what guise she would find him, "a vegetable seller" or "a freaky intellectual with a pipe and gray hair"; sometimes, only when he spoke to her would she recognize him. After almost four years on the run, he was captured and imprisoned. By that time, Nadia's mother had also been jailed for refusing to provide clues to his whereabouts. For three years husband and wife were in the same facility. He was tortured "a lot," Nadia says, and, at least once, they made her mother watch.

Later he was moved for two years to a remote prison, where inmates often did not survive. Such amenities as family visits were prohibited, except when bribes were forthcoming. Nadia's grandfather, she says, "paid a fortune," just for the privilege of seeing his son once a year. After two years he was moved to another prison—a "resort by comparison"—where he remained until at last released. He'd been in prison for 16 years.

Nadia's earliest memories of her father are confused, though she does remember visiting him in jail when she was five or six. And then, when she was about nine years old, he started smuggling messages to her "about how he's living, how he's surviving, how he thinks about the future." The notes were written in tiny script on cigarette paper—she needed a magnifying glass to read them. The most painful message came when she was a senior in high school. Until that year, she had been an outstanding student. But then, she says, the pressure of school became too much for her—she stopped studying, she missed exams, her grades plummeted. From prison her father wrote, "I want you to be one of the top always. I need that as a compensation for all the deprivation I've lived." She read the message over and over and could not stop crying. And then she thought, "I can never give him compensation for all that he's been through. I can't have such a responsibility."

Today, although Nadia cannot escape her family's past, she does not want to be consumed by it. "I have to detach myself from old history," she says, "to take a break. I need to be myself, not my father's daughter."

When Bashar al-Assad, a Western-educated ophthalmologist, came to power in 2000, after his father's death, people had high hopes of a "Damascus spring." In his inaugural address, Bashar spoke of "democracy" and "transparency," and, in fact, new freedoms did seem to blossom. Private newspapers were established; salons or forums for political discussion sprang up in people's homes; hundreds of political prisoners were released; and the infamous "Mezze" prison was closed. But then in response to threats both external and internal Bashar seemed to backtrack, for instance by shutting down forums and arresting their leaders. By 2004, Amnesty International was describing horrendous conditions in Syrian prisons and reporting that most techniques of torture used under Bashar's father continued to be practiced and that new ones had been introduced. Today, whatever Bashar's intentions may originally have been, there is, at best, confusion about the limits of free speech and political action.

As a result, most people tend to be circumspect in their statements and behavior. Roland told me about "a couple of average Syrians," friends he'd made early on when looking for an apartment. They sometimes talked politics with him but visited him only late at night, asked that most lights be turned off, and refused to step out on the balcony. Being on too-friendly terms with an American might make them suspect, or so they thought. "They're very nervous," Roland said, "about my neighbors reporting them to the secret police."

What one fears may never come to pass, may in fact be unlikely, but it is the fear itself, the paranoia deliberately cultivated by the powers that be, that keeps most people from stepping out of line. Even at the university. In my first and only real conversation with the chair of the English Department, she spelled out ground rules for my class: no readings to be assigned that were critical of Syria and none that praised Israel. In a class on American poetry and drama (think Robert Frost and Tennessee Williams), it was unlikely these topics would arise, but she wasn't taking any chances. She didn't want this stranger from America bringing trouble down on her head.

Given this political atmosphere, I was surprised at what I found when I picked up a copy of *Syria Today*, a glossy English-language magazine published in Damascus. It carried a cover story on the Melis Report, summarizing its findings in some detail and making no attempt to challenge its conclusions. To me it seemed a good, objective piece of journalism. The managing editor of *ST* is Betsy's former roommate Brooke, whom I'd met that evening at Mazen's. One day Brooke and I got together at a café she knew of across the street from the Japanese embassy, close enough that I could walk to it. Arabic music played in the background; at the next table, two young women, one bare-headed, one scarved, sat together having coffee.

ST comes out every four to six weeks. For each issue, Brooke carries the master to printers in Beirut, spends the night in the city, and brings the stacks of magazines back the next day. Then the censors at the Syrian Ministry of Education take a look. "Have they ever prevented distribution?" I asked. "No," she said and offered a couple of possible explanations. "First," she said, "the writing does require a fairly good grasp of the subtleties of English." In that sense, the government bureaucrats may not be up to the job. "Secondly," she said, "because it's in English, it's less available to the average Syrian reader." In other words, the government may give more leeway to a publication that, to begin with, most of its people cannot read.

In point of fact, *ST* is designed not so much for Syrians as for foreign diplomats and businessmen residing in the country and for an

English-speaking audience abroad. The goal, Brooke says, is "to provide a much fairer analysis of what goes on in Syria than foreigners might read in other magazines or newspapers. We want to encourage them to see Syria as an opportunity for investment. People think that Syria is a tiny little backwater with veiled women and angry men; they don't know there's a wealth of young and enthusiastic people here, who are educated."

Interested as I was in *ST*, I was equally intrigued by Brooke herself. Like Betsy, Theresa, and Deborah, she is what I've called a "freelancer," but it was neither romance nor war that had brought her to the region. A native of Australia, she had been living in England after completing a degree in military history that had whetted her interest in Crusader architecture, and so she signed up for a bus tour through Syria to see Krak de Chevalier (according to T.E. Lawrence, "the finest castle in the world") and other ancient sites. "I just absolutely fell in love," she says. "That whole epic quality here, like a completely exotic other world." Most people on vacation who are enchanted by romantic places find that memories suffice. They go home with photos to show and adventures to tell, but, otherwise, they pick up their lives where they've left off. Not Brooke. She took a course in teaching English as a foreign language, returned to Damascus, and got a job. (Though she soon moved on to her position at *ST*, Brooke still volunteers as a teacher in a Palestinian youth camp.)

Before we went our separate ways that afternoon (Brooke to her kickboxing class, I to pick up a half kilo of almonds on my way home), our conversation veered back to matters of censorship, freedom of expression, and docility toward those in authority. "In Australia," she says, "it's okay to say the prime minister is a dickhead. You can spray paint it on a wall, you can write it with a pen on a table, no one cares." Syrians wonder, she says, "Why can't we do that here?"

It seems plausible that as Syrians gain more information about the rest of the world, they may question how things are done at home.

When Bashar Assad, who had once been president of the Syria Computer Society, came to power, one of his early moves was to expand Internet access. Up to that point, it had been limited to government figures and certain others; perhaps 30,000 individuals were online. Today it is one million. But, like so many other signs of a Damascus spring, the promise of the Internet has not been fully realized. In 2006, Reporters Without Borders identified Syria as one of the worst offenders against Internet freedom. They charged the government with filtering content, monitoring e-mail, and, on occasion, shutting down blogs and arresting those who run them or read them. And yet one can point to web sites that explore social problems in Syria, don't faithfully parrot the government line, and still survive. In a burst of enthusiasm, one observer has even called the Internet an "unprecedented haven for public discourse [in Syria]." The problem seems again to be the challenge of predicting when the government will decide that such-and-such a statement crosses the line. Inconsistency is the hobgoblin.

One Syria-focused blog that went on line in 2004 is Syriacomment.doc, written by Joshua Landis, an American who teaches Middle Eastern history at the University of Oklahoma and visits Syria as often as he can. He is, in fact, married to a Syrian woman he met one summer in Damascus. When our paths crossed, he (together with wife and child) had been in the country for a year, on a Fulbright that overlapped with mine. Mostly political commentary, Syriacomment has attracted a good deal of attention. Joshua told me that, over the previous 12 months, he'd been quoted in more than a thousand articles and been interviewed on major American TV networks as well as on the BBC. "Every reporter who comes to town calls me," he said, "because [I'm] somebody who speaks English and who's following the politics day-to-day." Joshua even hears from reporters in the States, who want "to get the lay of the land."

It's crucial too that Joshua can do better than just get by in Arabic.

When he was very small, his father's job took the family to Saudi Arabia, where Joshua picked up a little of the language in nursery school. The next stop was Lebanon, where they lived in "a kind of golden ghetto," populated by Westerners and where he lost the bits of Arabic he'd learned. But, once his family returned to the States he was launched on what he calls "a normal American upbringing."

Then, after college, a teaching job took him again to Lebanon, where he "got interested in trying to figure out why people were killing each other and who the factions were and what was going on." A Fulbright fellowship in Syria followed, then a master's at Harvard in Middle Eastern Studies and a Ph.D. from Princeton. All the while, he was working on his Arabic, but it was only during this most recent year in Damascus that he had achieved true fluency. "To go to a dinner party where it's only Arabic being spoken and be relaxed and not get exhausted after half an hour—for 25 years, that's something I've been working for, and so to do it feels very gratifying."

I thought of my own attempts to improve my Arabic—a class I'd taken at Harvard; long conversations with my driver in Lebanon who knew just three words of English; and now my private lessons in Damascus. Tutoring aside, the longer I was in Syria, the more vocabulary and idiom came back to me, tapping into something primitive as childhood, transporting me to living rooms where my father and his friends drank Turkish coffee and argued politics, to kitchens where my mother and her sisters-in-law talked Ladies' Aid business as they chopped parsley and stuffed grape leaves.

Like Brooke, Joshua reported that he has encountered no overt government interference and no intimidation even though he is, in his words, "quite honest about dictatorship in Syria and lack of freedoms." His explanation was much like Brooke's, namely that the security people have little capability in English and that most Syrians have little access to what he writes. (In his case, not just because it is in English but because it is on the web rather than in print.) Other factors that probably work to his advantage—he's married to a Syrian Alawite, the minority religious sect to which the president's family belongs, and he has written pieces, such as an op-ed for the *New York Times*, that were considered pro-Syrian. "That won me some good will from people in the government here," he says. His "pro-Syrian" argument came down to this: "America's got to think two, three times before they come crashing in here because this is a complex society that could easily crumble into chaos. Or before they try to strangle Syria with sanctions."

When I last spoke to Joshua, he was just a couple of weeks away from heading back to Oklahoma. It had been an *annus mirabilis*. Syriacomment had taken off in a big way, at long last he was fully comfortable in Arabic, he'd made friends of writers and artists, his expertise had been called on by journalists and diplomats—all this a far cry from the life he'd experienced as an American academic. In his private life, he'd also gotten to know his in-laws well and that, he said, had been "a total joy."

"So it's going to be hard to leave?" I ventured.

"Oh, it's going to be misery. But a real motivation to find my way back."

THE UNIVERSITY

"Will you be back next year?" When I said no, a girl in the front row frowned. "We like you," she said.

Less goodwill came my way from colleagues and administrators at the university. My chair—harried or indifferent, I still don't know which—set the tone: not responding to repeated e-mails; not telling me when classes were cancelled for a holiday or a political demonstration; and, in all my weeks there, never introducing me to another soul. So much, I thought, for Arab hospitality. After a while, a kind of desperation set in. I telephoned Rana, an instructor whom I knew only by name; a friend had put me on to her. "You haven't met anyone in the department? You don't have an office or a key?" Rana sounded appropriately appalled and promised to catch up with me the next day after class, or the day after that. She never showed. Midway through the term, I did finally reach my chair on her cell phone. "I love the students and the teaching," I told her, "but I'd like to get to know more Syrians. Do you know of anyone who might like to meet me?" She thought for about two seconds before saying "No."

I wondered: "Is the problem here that I'm an American?" But Larry and Raili were asked over for dinner by faculty in the School of Agriculture, taken on sight-seeing excursions, invited to weddings. I couldn't help but think too of how different things had been in Beirut when I'd been on a similar Fulbright grant to the Lebanese University. There, the chair of the department had spent an afternoon helping me look for an apartment, she'd taken me out to lunch, she'd invited me to her parents' home in the mountains. Another colleague, who'd come along on the house-hunting expedition, took me to meet the Minister of Education. He'd laughed at my American-accented Arabic but picked up the tab for a visit to Lebanon's stunning Jeita Grotto, followed by a lavish lunch, and also arranged for a private tour of the national museum; through the efforts of yet another colleague, I was invited to address classes at the American University of Beirut, the country's premier institution of higher learning.

In Lebanon, the American embassy too had felt a sense of responsibility for my well being. One aide called me every week to see how I was doing, the cultural affairs attaché invited me along on a visit to the opening of an art exhibit and an evening at a jazz club. I was asked to Thanksgiving dinner at the embassy, and, before I left the country, the chargé d'affaires hosted a farewell dinner in my honor. At the embassy in Damascus, a different ethos prevailed. I was pretty much expected to look out for myself, although one Syrian employee took me for a quick peek at a vacant apartment, and an

American on the staff lent me several books. Both gestures were kind since in neither case was I that person's responsibility. When I asked the woman charged with supervising Fulbrights the same question I'd asked my chair—could she think of any Syrians to introduce me to—I got the same answer: "No."

My students were a different story. In fact, a delight. We met in an auditorium that held about 300 people and that, on the first day of class, was nearly full. As the semester progressed, the class thinned out, but usually 75 to 100 showed up. I used a hand-held microphone. Given the size of the class, the chair had warned me not to expect much discussion. "It's all lecture," she said. But it turned out that a number of students—especially those who regularly claimed the front rows—were eager to talk. They'd done the reading and had questions to ask. "Is this an example of existentialism?" "Is this like the chorus in a Greek play?" "Is this what you call the theater of the absurd?" They wanted, almost desperately, to understand.

I remember, especially, a young man who dreamed of being a playwright. He brought in a one-act drama he'd written and had privately published. (Like everything printed in Syria, it had to be okayed by government censors.) The play was derivative, smacking of Albee, but it showed talent and seriousness of purpose. He wanted to study in the States—I helped him find information on drama programs—but he worried that Americans would hate him for being Arab. Another student, a Kurd, planned to pursue a graduate degree in anthropology; he already had an irresistible topic for a master's thesis, a study of his father and older men in his family who made a living smuggling goods across the border with Turkey. Then there was the boy who took umbrage at one of my questions. We'd been reading *The Glass Menagerie*. "Imagine it takes place in Damascus," I said. "How would a Syrian mother try to marry off her daughter? Would a Syrian son desert his family to follow his own star?" In short, I wanted to know how the play might be altered to ring true to Syrian society. The young man who spoke up was vehement: "We have the same feelings, we are not different." I still think my line of questioning was legitimate and might have led to exploration of cultural differences. But clearly he had heard something else in my words or my tone. Perhaps condescension or an implication that Syrians could be reduced to stereotypes. Another boy rose in support of his class-mate. "Even if this family is Syrian, you don't have to change a word."

I remember too the little acts of kindness—the girl who ran to the bookstore to get me a copy of the textbook I hadn't known existed, the boy who without being asked set up my microphone at the start of each class, the girls who hailed taxis for me, another girl who rode the bus with me to my stop, showing me the way, even though as I later learned she lived in another direction.

And then the students who asked me to write letters supporting their applications to study in the States. With little to go on, especially if the student asking was quiet in class, it could be a challenge. Still, I'd rack my brain to come up with anything that might help. I didn't want to say no, realizing what a precious opportunity it would be for any one of my students to go abroad and suspecting too that other instructors probably knew even less about them than I did. "The professors, they don't talk to us," I was told. Which, if true, helped account for the crowd of students that pressed up to ask me questions after every class. One girl for whom I wrote a recommendation was working against a deadline, so I had her pick up the letter at my flat. Fifteen minutes later, my door bell buzzed again. She'd returned bearing an armload of roses, lilies, and *zumbaq*, a cream-colored flower—native to Syria—with an intoxicating scent. This is what it's like, I thought, to live in a society where the give-and-take of personal relations is paramount and honor resides in open-handedness.

As for the content of my course, it was pretty much my call, as long as I adhered to the requirement that all readings be American poetry or drama. A requirement interpreted rigidly as I discovered when I mentioned to the chair at that early meeting that in teaching a one-act play by the Provincetown writer Susan Glaspell, I'd like also to assign the play's later incarnation as a short story. I thought I had an excellent rationale: "To show the differences in the genres." "No," she said, "they read fiction *next* year." Otherwise, except for avoiding politically charged material, I could—when it came to content—do as I pleased. But not when it came to work I could expect from my students. Given, I suppose, the size of classes, I was not to make written assignments or to give any quizzes or exams. I later heard that, even in writing courses, students were not expected to produce essays.

Pedagogically speaking, I couldn't say much for that approach. But it did make my life a lot easier—no papers to read or exams to grade. More important, no occasion for tension or hard feeling between me and my students. No pleas to nudge a B plus into an A. Of course, students did walk away with a grade for the course, but it depended entirely on a final exam, which had to have a specified number of questions, all multiple-choice. A machine would do the grading. I was instructed to make up two such exams, one to be administered at the end of the semester, the other a make-up for those who failed the first. A multiple-choice test in a literature course—I'd never done or thought of doing such a thing. It wasn't easy. And I wasn't sure that it was fair. I began to worry that students who had excelled all semester might somehow fall short.

When I dropped off the test questions at the department office, the chair happened to be at her desk. Now was my opportunity. "Can I have some input into the final grades?" I asked her. "Can I boost the grade of someone who's done well all term?" She was shocked at the suggestion. Later, when I thought about it, I understood her probable reasoning—the grading was to be totally objective, un-colored by bias or personal feeling. (I'd heard that, in the old days, professors in some departments regularly sold grades for sex.) Still, the system didn't sit right with me. I kept my fingers crossed that the most thoughtful and responsible students would ace the exam.

A few weeks after I'd returned to the States, I got an e-mail from one of my Syrian students—the one, in fact, who'd taken me to Mazen's party. "I thought you'd like to know," he wrote. "The grades have been posted. In our class, out of 1600 students, 400 didn't pass." Sixteen hundred students! Who? Where? I remembered a young man who had come up to me after class one day, with a question about what the final exam would cover. He didn't look familiar. "Have you been to class before?" I asked. "No," he said. "Well, will you be coming from now on?" He looked at me strangely. "I live in Aleppo," he said. Now, with that e-mail in front of me, I understood that he was not an anomaly and that I had laid eyes on only a minority of the students enrolled in my course.

The question, one might think, is not why did 400 fail but how did 1200 pass? The answer lies in a system, the workings of which it took me a while to piece together. From almost the first class, I noticed that a couple of students had tape recorders on their desks. As they got to know me better, they confided that they were not taping for their own benefit; rather, they were employed, each by a different bookstore, to record lectures and whatever they could pick up of class discussion and then to transcribe the tapes. The bookstores sold the transcripts to students who did not or could not attend class and, I suppose, to others looking for a backup to their own class notes. "Can I see a copy?" I asked one of the students. "Of course," he said and brought me in a stack of booklets, one for each class meeting. To tell the truth, I was surprised. Inevitably, there were errors and misunderstandings, but, on the whole, the transcripts gave a decent enough sense of lecture and class discussion. One of the two transcribers had even gone so far as to supplement the tapes with his own online research. Thinking back, then, yes, I could see it. Students who studied those transcripts probably could manage to pick off the correct answer to half the questions on the exam, which was all that was required in order to pass.

GENDER, SEX, AND THE VEIL

On the last day of class I brought in a camera. As I look now at the photos, the bright eyes, the frank smiles, the boys in their T-shirts and jeans, the girls in their long sleeves and head scarves, I remember my surprise on arriving in Damascus. Beforehand, insofar as I'd thought about it at all, I'd expected to find what I'd seen in neighboring Lebanon, most females in Western-style dress. True, a scattering of girls in my class did go bare-headed, but they were exceptions (as was the girl who wore a black veil over her face, exposing only her eyes). The interesting thing was that the mass of girls who had elected to wear the *hijab* were not necessarily following in their mothers' footsteps. As in many parts of the world, a religious revival had swept up the younger generation or, in some cases, caused middle-aged women to dress more conservatively than they had 20 years earlier.

Samia, a grade-school teacher, is one of those women. As she tells it, her mother and her sister, neither of whom wears the scarf, don't take their faith seriously enough. "I study my religion," she said, "and I work at it." Her conclusion: "God wants women to cover their hair." The full-length *abaya* is a different matter—"That's not Islamic," she said, arguing that one has to distinguish between religious dictate and cultural tradition. The more I listened to Samia, the more she seemed the perfect antidote to the stereotype of the downtrodden Arab woman; well-versed in her faith, sure of her ground, quick to set people straight. For instance, the Muslim man who refused to shake hands with her (she told him that pollution came not from a woman's touch but from "what was in his own heart"), the policeman in Saudi Arabia who threatened her with a stick because her face was unveiled (she wrestled back his arm until he let her go), and the nun who tried to bar her entry to a church (Samia insisted that she too believed in the Prophet Jesus and quietly walked in to pray).

As the last example shows, Samia's impulses—devout Muslim though she may be—are ecumenical. One day, she suggested to her students that they create an ideal community. "What shall we put in it?" she asked, as she stood at the blackboard, chalk at the ready. One boy suggested a mosque. When the other students laughed because that boy was Christian, she came up with the idea of a single building that could function as both mosque and church. At first, there were objections. The Muslim students couldn't tolerate "all those pictures you find in churches." She asked the Christian boy if he needed to have pictures: "No." She asked the Muslim students if they could live with candles. "Yes, that would be nice."

Mai is a younger Muslim woman, a graduate of the American University of Beirut. On the day we met, we stopped for cappuccino and fresh fruit at an Italian restaurant that looked to have an international clientele. The kind of place where Mai—fresh from cosmopolitan Beirut—could relax. It had been hard, she said, coming back to Damascus and its more intense religious climate. Girlfriends, who had never done so before, were now wearing the *hijab* and generally dressing more conservatively. Mai's clothes—jeans, a sweater with a scoop neck—looked like those that an American student might wear. Friends scolded her; one warned that, if she didn't change her ways, she would go to hell.

Still, Mai's garb was downright prudish compared to what I sometimes spotted at the university—sequined tops; skin-tight, hip hugger jeans; and spike-heeled plastic boots in incandescent colors. I assumed the few girls teetering around in these outfits were Christian, that no Muslim girl would dare go so far. But Judith told me that a few did dress just as provocatively although, incongruous as it seems, they might still conceal their hair. Actually, there were times when, simply out of vanity, I would gladly have concealed my own. In fact, one day when I couldn't bear it any longer, I did what I'd occasionally done at home: I wrapped a striped scarf around my head, bringing the ends together in what I hoped was a stylish bow. In the States, my students hadn't given it a second glance. But as I entered my classroom in Damascus, the boys stared; the girls exchanged whispers and, courteous as they were, tried not to laugh out loud. I'm not sure what they saw or thought they saw or thought I meant, but I never wore a scarf to class again.

Female dress, I decided, was a complicated matter, governed by codes I didn't entirely fathom and sending messages it wasn't always easy to decipher. For instance, those girls who slathered on makeup and dressed like tarts—what were they announcing? "Not what you might think," one woman told me. "Those clothes are a sublimation, a substitute for normal boy-girl relations." In other words, I wasn't to leap to any conclusions about overheated sex lives. How these girls might act in private settings, I couldn't know, but I did notice that, between classes, they almost never hung out with boys. Instead, they strolled and sat and chatted with other girls who might or might not dress as they did. On campus, informal segregation by gender was the norm. (And yet my tutor was astonished when I told him that I'd graduated from a women's college. "In Saudi, we expect such things," he said. "But in America?")

The mix of girls and boys in class, I supposed, could easily lead to romantic involvement though I detected no clear evidence of it. Nor did I want to pry. I did ask once, "What does it mean if a boy and girl walk together on campus?" "Just friends," my students shot back. Their tone was indignant, as if warding off the suspicions of petty minds. One way or another, of course, girls and boys do get acquainted, whether at university, at weddings, through their families, or because they're neighbors. One evening in Baab Touma, when I was waiting on the street for a friend, I saw mixed groups of young people congregate in the plaza, then hurry off, presumably to restaurants, coffee houses, or one of the new discos. (In other sections of the city, other girls and boys, both Muslim and Christian, might be doing the same.) I remembered my parents' rule—no dates, no pairing off, but going out with a crowd was safe and respectable.

I remembered too my parents' preference that I keep an eye out for a nice Lebanese young man. Or some variety of Arab. But in America they knew such a match was not necessarily in the cards. Already, my older cousins were harbingers of disappointment; they'd married third-generation Americans, two with Irish, one with German, and one with Italian roots. My aunt and uncle weren't angry, only a little melancholy that their traditions and heritage were being watered down. In Syria, parents took such defections more seriously. They might tolerate a flirtation between their sons and visiting Western women, but marriage was a harder pill to swallow. Brooke told me about her girlfriend, also Australian, who was dating a Syrian man. At first, his parents said, "You can't have anything to do with her"; then it was, "Okay, you can see her, but we don't want to meet her"; now that wall has also showed signs of cracking—ever since the father was forced to turn to the girl for help with a letter he had to write in English.

Even when boy and girl are both Syrian, they are not necessarily home free; the bias against religiously mixed marriages can be unyielding. I told Brooke about a case I'd heard of in Baab Touma, where a Christian girl married a Muslim. Her family murdered her, her husband, and his family. Brooke told me about a Druze girl who secretly married a Christian. When she worked up the courage to tell her family, they said, "Come home, we're going to have a big wedding, everything's going to be great." They killed her on her "wedding" day.

"And yet," Brooke said, "one of the great things that you feel about Syria—from a historical perspective it's certainly true—is that the

131

three major religions [Christian, Muslim, and Jewish] have lived here happily, side by side. Taxi drivers will tell you, *We are all brothers, we all worship the same God.* But, under the surface, it's *we won't let our children intermix or interbreed."* (For the Christian community to survive in Syria, my tutor said, "we cannot marry Muslims.") Of course, as Brooke herself readily admits, and as her own experience illustrates, not every Syrian family is dead set against interfaith marriage. And, of those who are, it's fair to say that only a few would resort to bloodshed. The horror stories Brooke and I swapped are profoundly distressing but I think not typical.

Marriage aside, the taboo against unmarried girls having sex with anyone—Western or Syrian, Christian or Muslim—is still strong. "If you were Syrian," Brooke said, "you could not check into a hotel room with a person of the opposite sex unless you showed a marriage certificate." She asked me if I'd noticed men "hanging around" hotel corridors. "They're just making sure," she said, "that people are not running in and out of each other's rooms." Still, she said, some young people manage to have intimate relations. "But I really don't know where they're doing it."

Mary—blonde, attractive, middle-aged—brought a different per-spective to bear. Wherever she went, she drew attention; married men of her acquaintance might ask her out. At first, she "freaked," but Syrian women friends calmed her down. "If you don't want to do it, don't do it," one said, "but it's very common." By which she meant that married men do have affairs. For that matter, so do women. Of course, being foreign made Mary—or so men might assume—a more likely candidate for an amour. "As a Western woman," she said, "you need to make your choice as to whether that's something that you will or won't do. And I'm not casting judgment either way."

It would be impossible—certainly for me—to say whether Christian or Muslim spouses are more apt to stray. It may matter that some Muslim men who can afford it still take second wives. (Does that make them less likely to enter into extramarital dalliances?). It may matter that among Christians, divorce is rare. (Are men and women mired in unhappy marriages more likely to pursue illicit liaisons?) Divorced, herself, Mary wonders, "What's the point to staying married to someone for 50 years if you're miserable? Muslims," she notes with approval, "are able to say, *this isn't working.*"

RELIGION

During the holy month of Ramadan, observant Muslims practice self-denial from dawn to dusk—no food or drink, no smokes, no sex. Burrowed under my blankets, the sky still dark, I'd waken to the haunting chant of the muezzin. I might not make out the prayers, but I supplied my own sub-text: "Long day ahead. Up now and eat while you can." Something comforting about that voice, I thought, reminding sleepy-eyed believers that they were not alone. Across the neighborhood, across the city, and—give or take a few hours—throughout the world, others were embarking on the same spiritual journey. Feeling strangely content myself, I'd tug the bed clothes tighter and drift off, though I might stir again at first light, when cannon signaled the beginning of the fast.

During Ramadan, life in Syria adapts to meet the needs of the faithful, and I had to adapt, too. Classes at the university met earlier in the day so that students could be back with their families by dusk; no more long, lingering breakfasts for me. On days I didn't teach, if I went out at noon looking for a restaurant, I'd find that most were closed. Afternoons, I had to get at my shopping before merchants locked up; like everyone else—students, cab drivers, office workers, laborers—they were eager to be home. When cannon sounded for the last time at the end of the day, they broke their fast with dates and water (as was the Prophet's habit) before sitting down to an elaborate *iftar* meal with family and friends. Like Thanksgiving, I thought, but one man took a more jaundiced view: "The way we stuff ourselves," he complained to me. "Is this how we learn to feel with the poor?"

The occasional Christian—mostly, I think, foreigners like Raili and Betsy—fasted in solidarity with their Muslim friends or as an exercise in self-discipline. The large majority who did not go that far, still watched themselves. Mindful of their neighbors' sensibilities, most avoided behaviors such as snacking in front of Muslim coworkers, chewing gum on the bus, or walking down the street smoking a cigarette. It's that degree of tact, I suppose, that has allowed these communities to coexist for centuries. Sometimes—or so it seemed to me—the two faiths actually clasp hands, as in Samia's reverence for the Prophet Jesus. More often, they seem like old-time neighbors standing on opposite sides of a street, acknowledging one another with a nod. I think now of an October day when I was visiting a Christian family in Baab Touma. We were sitting around the dinner table when my hostess said, "Listen," and I made out the distant boom of cannon. "Ramadan begins," she said. Five minutes later, without budging from our seats, we heard "Joy to the World" caroled by a local boys' choir. "Rehearsing for Christmas," I was told in the same calm tone of voice. As if this rubbing of elbows was a natural thing.

As Christmas approached, the streets of Baab Touma were decked out with lights, and restaurants were decorated. In one festive display, stuffed Santas were positioned on rope ladders overlooking the dining room at the center of which a fountain billowed with drifts of suds that looked like snow. For dessert, each table of diners was presented with a platter on which red and green scoops of ice cream had been arranged in a wreath. In celebration of the season, it was on the house.

Late in December, I attended a Christmas concert in a packed downtown theater. For an hour and a half, chorus and soloists performed a familiar repertoire of carols sung in Arabic, English, French, German, and, in one case, Aramaic (the language of Christ). Intermingled with the carols were seasonal songs that evoked the exotic: white Christmases, sleigh rides, snowmen, and a red-nosed reindeer. The concert concluded, as it surely would have in America, with "We wish you a merry Christmas," though it was sung first in Arabic and then in English. Only as we were leaving did I learn that most of the chorus were Muslim. It was a wonderful feel-good evening, especially for those of us who were far from home. But I did notice that, in the chorus's rendition of "The First Noel," one line had been changed. Instead of "Born is the king of Israel," they sang, "Born is the king Emmanuel." I wondered if it was the censor's hand at work.

One thing Syrians—indeed, all Arabs—share, regardless of religion, is a kind of fatalism (though that may not be quite the word). The conviction that God holds the universe in the cup of his hands, that not a sparrow falls. As Jim had noted, God's name is regularly invoked in everyday conversation, the most ubiquitous phrase being *n'shallah*, "God willing." I'd encountered it first at home. As a child, I'd overhear my mother on the phone with her cousin or her sister-in-law, making plans for the following day, arranging to go together to a meeting, a wake, or a church supper. The details worked out, she'd sign off with something like, "Good, we will meet then at seven, *n'shallah*." For years, I thought *n'shallah* was Arabic for "tomorrow."

It's almost impossible to overstate the hold that phrase or some variation of it has on Arabs, both Christian and Muslim. But when addressed to a literal-minded Westerner—even one who'd grown up as I had—it can sometimes shut down communication. Once I was trying to get straight the hours of my little neighborhood grocery. "You opened at 10 today," I said. The owner agreed. "But after Ramadan," I said, "will you open earlier?" "*N'shallah.*" Was that a maybe or a yes? Before heading out for a week's trip to Aleppo and points north, I took my jacket to the local tailor for mending. "I leave in two days," I said. "Will it be ready?" "*N'shallah*." "Please, I want to take it with me." "*N'shallah*." Push though I might for a promise, that was as far as he would go.

The point, of course, is that it would be impious to predict the future, to think that one can control events. This insistent deference to God's will is analogous to the custom that rug makers follow in the East, deliberately working one mistake into the weaving. To do otherwise would be arrogant since only God is perfect. As arrogant as promising that my jacket would be ready on a particular day. Every so often I realize that my early cultural training has never quite lost its hold. I don't pepper my conversation with "*n'shallah's*" but neither am I comfortable with sentences that begin "I will." Instead, I resort to spineless formulations like "My plan is" or "I expect to." Why provoke the gods to make plain to me who's boss?

One could argue that *n'shallah* is no more than a verbal tic, or a gesture about on a level with crossing one's fingers. But sometimes it's clearly more. I was in a cab on my way to the American embassy. The driver, sensing I was from the States, launched a political tirade against American policies in the region. I agreed where I could and kept mum where I couldn't. But his voice was rising and he was losing patience. "This is one angry man," I thought. Then, for a short space, he was silent, and I assumed he was marshalling new arguments or perhaps just thinking dark thoughts. But when he spoke again, his tone had changed. "After all," he said, catching my eye in his rearview mirror, "nothing happens except as God wills it." In a moment, he'd gone from agitated to serene.

LEBANESE AMERICAN

As an American, I was always conscious that I came from a place toward which most Syrians felt some degree of disapproval if not hostility. At the same time, I knew that many of these self-same critics also bought into the idea of the United States as a land of opportunity and personal freedom. That contradiction was brought home to me one morning when I saw a parade of young people, waving Syrian flags and chanting anti-Bush slogans, march down the hill in front of the American embassy; two hours later, some were back, standing in line outside the embassy door, waiting to apply for student visas to the United States

In wondering how I'd be received in Syria, I'd assumed my nationality would be self-evident, but, as it turned out, Syrians often had difficulty placing me. *French*, *German*, or even *Australian* were popular guesses. *American* did not immediately leap to mind. But, as soon as I opened my mouth in Arabic, they had the other strand of my heritage pegged. "Can you tell my family is Lebanese?" I asked the man selling guide books at the museum. "From the first word," he said.

American *and* Lebanese—a double whammy. Tensions between Syria and Lebanon were rising, fueled by the assassination of Rafic Hariri and the suspicion—in some quarters, the conviction—that Syria had masterminded it. I'd been invited to a December wedding in Beirut. To leave the country, I needed written permission from the university and the Syrian government; that is, if I intended (as I surely did) to come back and resume my teaching. After I'd heard from enough people that Americans and Lebanese might be hassled by Syrian officials at the border, I decided I couldn't risk exiting the country and then, on my return, being detained for hours. Still, I hoped that a couple of people I'd known in Lebanon would drive to Damascus, if only for the day, to visit me. One begged off politely. The other was more direct. "No," she e-mailed me. "We've had enough of Syria and Syrians."

Those Lebanese who felt as she did, were generally critical also of their own president, who was an ally—some would say a tool—of Syria. In fact, it's been argued that it was his election to a third term—in violation of the constitution but agreed to under pressure from the Syrians—that was the last straw for those already resentful of Syria's throwing its weight around in Lebanon. To be halted at checkpoints manned by Syrian soldiers was, for many Lebanese, not merely an irritation but an indignity.

On the other hand, Syrians I met were rarely critical of the Lebanese. Perhaps concern for my feelings made some bite their tongue, but others seemed actually to romanticize Lebanon. It was a longstanding habit; according to Theresa, her mother-in-law used to maintain that the air improved the moment she crossed the border. May, as I've suggested, sorely missed her student days in Beirut. A young man in my class told me that Lebanese were "more open-minded, more advanced." Two girls I ran into at a campus demonstration went on about how beautiful Beirut was. "But so is Damascus," I said. "Not like Beirut," they insisted, "not like Lebanon." Perhaps the most common sentiment I heard from Syrians, when speaking of the Lebanese, was this: "We are brothers, we are one people." It sounded friendly enough, but that last claim—"one people"—alarmed those Lebanese who feared that Syria had designs upon their country. As proof, they pointed to the odd fact that Syria has no embassy in Lebanon. Wasn't this, implicitly, an erasure of boundaries and a denial of Lebanese sovereignty?

To me, the notion that the two people were one was neither alien nor surprising. I'd grown up in an era when the great majority of Arab Americans—90 percent of whom were then from Lebanon—referred to themselves as "Syrians." From childhood through approximately my freshman year of college, that's who I was. My subsequent assumption of a Lebanese identity felt like an overlay until, by virtue of repetition, I internalized it. Of course, even when we called ourselves Syrians (in Arabic, *Suriyiin*), we made a distinction between ourselves—we who traced our ancestry to peasant villages in Mount Lebanon—and those others whom we called *shwaam*, an Arabic word for Damascenes. They were part of our ethnic family, to be sure, but a different branch. They had their own church, often their own clubs, and the immigrant generation (if not their children) mostly socialized among themselves. Still, they did make a point of attending our fund raisers—church dinners, picnics, Arabic movies—and, in turn, we patronized theirs.

As a child, I recognized the *shwaam* by their Arabic accent, a kind of drawl that, to my ears, sounded like an affectation, and by their women, who seemed to wear more make up than ours did as well as more gold bangles and fancier silk dresses. In short, as I now realize, the *shwaam* were citified. For their part, they—or some of them—looked down on us as country bumpkins. When my cousin wanted to marry a girl from the *shwaam* community, his father had a little talk with her before he'd give his blessing. He shook his finger in her face: "Don't ever let me hear you refer to us as *jabaliiyi* (mountain people)," he told her. *Jabaliiyi*, to his mind, being equivalent to "hillbillies."

Calling ourselves Syrian was not so perverse as it may at first appear. In the late 19th and early 20th centuries, when its people first emigrated, Mount Lebanon (though semi-autonomous) was embedded in Greater Syria, which was, itself, a province of the Turkish Ottoman empire. But after the Ottomans met defeat in the First World War, the European powers remapped the region. Mount Lebanon's borders ballooned west to capture ancient coastal cities (Beirut, Tripoli, Tyre, Sidon) and east, to swallow the fertile Bekaa Valley. By the time independence was gained in the forties, Lebanon and Syria had evolved into two separate, sovereign states although it would take a good decade or more for most immigrants from Lebanon and their children to shrug off their Syrian identity. (My father never did. Who, he demanded, gave these foreigners the right to carve up our lands?)

I've said that, in my presence, Syrians spoke tactfully about the Lebanese, and sometimes with what sounded like genuine enthusiasm.

But I also remember the hurt in my driver's voice when he suggested, without quite saying so, that the Lebanese were ungrateful for Syrian aid during their civil war. He himself had served in that action—he recalled how his mother had cried when he marched off to war—and he'd seen the decapitated bodies of comrades. From time to time, I heard more outspoken criticism of the Lebanese, almost always from Westerners on a mission (or so it seemed to me) to prove Syria's superiority. "Lebanon is so overrated," one told me. "I'd much rather be here." The usual line of attack went something like this: by contrast with Syria, Lebanon was too "Western," not "authentic," not "Arab" enough. And the women. They all went in for plastic surgery, draped themselves in French couture, and spent hours being pampered in hair and nail salons. One evening in Damascus, I spent some 20 minutes— all I could take—watching the Miss Lebanon beauty pageant on TV. In any country, such spectacles are hardly edifying, but there was something more than usually disquieting about these young women who injected French or English into every sentence, as if Arabic lacked the legs to stand up on its own. Another day I heard a joke about a demonstration in Beirut at which well heeled ladies showed up with their maids. According to the story, one maid held up a sign that read, "Madame demands . . . ."

There was a seed of truth to all the mockery. I'd heard Lebanese, in frustration, say pretty much the same. But they were directing their complaints at a particular segment of their society; the mockers I met in Syria were taking that segment for the whole. (They might have done better to point to Lebanon's savage civil war. That—not frivolity or conspicuous consumption—was the dark stain on the nation.) When I thought back to people I had known in Lebanon, it was their wit and energy that sprang to mind, their improbable *joie de vivre*. Traits of a piece with the resourcefulness that has underwritten the survival of their society. Though, of late, just barely.

I hadn't guessed that Syria would be so seductive or that it would challenge the hold that Lebanon had on my affections. Two Fulbrights, two neighboring countries, but in one case a set of circumstances that worked to claim me.

In Beirut, I camped out in a hotel suite, ate breakfast in the dining room, went out for dinner (or ordered room service), had my linens laundered and my rooms cleaned by the staff, had a driver waiting across the street to drive me to school and back. In Damascus, I bantered with shopkeepers in my broken Arabic, cooked stews, brewed Turkish coffee, washed soot off the floors of my apartment, learned where to dispose of my kitchen garbage, coped with power failures and, once, a flooded bathroom. (Do not put tissue in the toilet, my landlord instructed me, after the fact.) In short, I pursued a daily routine that approximated that of my neighbors. (Though no one ever mistook me for a native.) In Lebanon, on the other hand—despite having a cousin down the street—I could seldom shake my role as tourist or privileged visitor from abroad. The very fact that the embassy and department kept a solicitous eye on me meant that I had less occasion to fend for myself and, therefore, less opportunity to play the role of a Beiruti. Given the cosmopolitan character of the city, I also had less need to crank my creaky Arabic into action.

Then too, though I was the only Fulbright in all of Lebanon, I was just one of many Americans and, as such—except for embassy personnel and my colleagues at the university—excited no special interest. In Syria, it was the opposite. I belonged to a cohort of Americans on government grants who helped me gain my footing and widened my circle of acquaintances. But, in the larger scheme of things, our numbers were still so few that, wherever I went, I was an object of eager and—almost always—friendly interest.

Lebanon and Syria, it's a balancing act. Cousin vs. cousin, charm vs. charm. At heart, I am still rooted in the villages of Mount Lebanon that shaped my parents' humor, idiom, and ethics, and drove the current of their imagination. Their culture is my context. Upon a time, I thought to slip its bonds, but, like Tom in *The Glass Menagerie*, I am more faithful than I meant to be.

But I also have a wandering eye. Damascus—no point denying it—swept me off my feet. "It casts its spell on you," Brooke said. "You feel, *I have to come back, I want to stay.*" Long before I said my good-byes, I knew exactly what she meant.

ALBUM

I've taken a bus to the southern town of Bosra, then walked along a path to the Roman amphitheater, which is one of Syria's architectural treasures. Encased inside a citadel, it has survived the centuries. A poster of Bashar al-Assad, perhaps four stories high, hangs above the entry.

Every day, men in uniform are stationed under trees outside the American Cultural Center. They sit on chairs, drinking coffee and concentrating on a black and white TV. Sometimes it's news that's on, sometimes it's soap opera. "They are guarding us," a Syrian woman in the office tells me. "At least, I think so."

Young men, weapons slung over their shoulder, patrol the sidewalk in front of the American embassy. I ring a doorbell and flash my ID so that the guard inside can see it through the little window in the door. He lets me in. Several months later, back in America, I recognize that very door in a photo on the front page of my newspaper. It is the spot at which gunmen have attacked the embassy. A security guard has been killed—could it be the one who finally got to know my face?—and a number of bystanders have been wounded.

I'm out to dinner with a group of visiting women who teach schoolchildren at an American naval base in the Gulf. They've come to Syria to sightsee. Apropos of nothing, one of them begins to sing the praises of the late Israeli prime minister Golda Meir. "I wouldn't say that around here, if I were you," I tell her. She looks puzzled.

A Saudi Arabian woman living in Damascus used to peddle Avon cosmetics and Victoria's Secret lingerie. Now, I'm told, she relies on agents. They get their percentage, she gets hers. Business is good.

I'm on a group excursion, and it's well past noon. I ask the man beside me on the bus if he's getting hungry. "Yes," he says in Arabic, "the birds in my belly are twittering."

At Mazen's, an American woman insists on speaking to me in Arabic. What's the point? Her Arabic isn't good, and mine is far from fluent. The effort makes me tired.

I meet a Polish girl at a dinner party. She announces she's engaged to a tennis player from St. Petersburg, which is why she's studying not just Arabic but Russian. "He's very famous," she says and names him. But it turns out she's never met the man, just watches his matches on TV. "I *could* marry him," she insists. "Anything is possible." And so she studies hard.

I'm in a bakery, buying spinach pies which, as I know from previous experience, will be delicious. "Do you make them here?" I ask the man who waits on me. He turns and shouts—three young men troop in from behind the scenes. Bashful, not sure if they're being teased. One says, "I make the stuffing." He says it softly, but he wants me to know. When the three withdraw again to the kitchen, the man at the counter pulls out a book and holds it up so I can see. The title reads, *American English*. "I study," he whispers.

I'm sitting at a table in the campus coffee house, invited there by Yusuf, a graduate student in philosophy, and his friend Sleiman, who is pre-med. Both dream of continuing their studies in the States. I know what's coming, a request for help in getting there—why else have they taken me up? I rehearse an answer that boils down to: "Not much I can do." They ask would I like another cup of coffee, but I have no time. They escort me to my classroom, shake my hand, and wish me a safe journey home.

I am standing in front of a newspaper kiosk on Abu-Roumana, hoping for a *Herald Trib*. A young man walks by, hand in hand with a middle-aged woman who must be his mother. They are chatting and laughing like friends.

Two old men stand on the sidewalk in earnest conversation. One has his right arm on the other's shoulder; his left hand plays with worry beads.

On a corner near my mosque, a mother is scolding her young daughter. The girl scowls and digs her toe into a patch of weeds. I hear my mother's voice, same intonation, same words. *Haji ta'imli hayk*—"Stop it now, behave!"

I am walking down Nuri Basha, watching my step on the uneven pavement. I hear a voice and look up to see a woman in a doorway. Across the street her daughter, nine or 10 years old, hair in a pony tail, is heading for the store where I buy bread and, in my weaker moments, candy. "What?" the woman calls out in Arabic. "Aren't you there *yet*?" The girl gives a saucy glance over her shoulder and makes a point of slowing down.

I am climbing the stairs to my flat. Ahead are a woman and her two daughters. Though they live just one floor below me, I have never met them. As the mother unlocks her door, she turns and sees me. "*Tfaddali*," she says, gesturing for me to enter. "Please do us the honor." For an instant, I'm not sure which would be ruder, to impose on her hospitality or to refuse it. "*Shukran*," I say, "Thank you," and continue on my way. Her blessing follows me up the stairs. *Allah ma'ik*, "God be with you."

Winter has arrived, I make chicken soup, I sweep rain water from my balcony.

Back in Boston. It's been two weeks, and I'm still on a high. Standing in a museum, admiring a Cézanne, I rest my hand on my chest. Something there. Days later, I know for sure; after 30 years, my cancer has returned. I hug my memories of Damascus tight.

———•••———

AFTERMATH (SUMMER 2008)

Since my return from Syria in early 2006, some things there have changed; other things have turned out not to be as they then seemed. Take Joshua Landis's statement that he'd encountered no government interference in his blogging, no attempts to intimidate or silence him. He has since discovered that, all along, the Syrian *mukhabarat* or secret police were tracking his site quite closely. During the summer of 2007, when he was again in Syria, the government issued an order to expel him, a document that was rescinded only through the inter-vention of the Syrian ambassador to the United States who happened to be in Damascus at the time. And even the ambassador, Joshua told me, "had to appeal all the way up to the palace."

The following spring (2008), Roland was refused entry into Syria despite his having a valid visa. In all probability, the reason was that Roland, still on the career diplomatic track, was now working for the State Department. Joshua explains this cracking down as part of a "tit-for-tat" war that has emerged between Syria and the United States. In Washington, Syrian officials are harassed, and the Syrian embassy cannot get a FAX hookup to work.

And then there is the matter of personal safety. I regularly tell my friends that, nowhere, at home or abroad, have I felt less threat-ened than in Damascus. But over the last year I have received reports suggesting that public spaces have become more dangerous. Theresa wrote me about an 86-year-old woman "mugged in broad daylight at the entrance to her house, on a very busy street." Brooke told me about a woman in her seventies, sitting in her car when she was assaulted—"punched in the face by a guy with a knife, trying to get her bag." Again, this incident took place in the middle of the day in a "safe" neighborhood.

This increase in street crime has its roots in a changing economy. According to Brooke, prices have doubled since I left Syria, a state of affairs that has created "plenty of desperate people." Joshua explains that policies to liberalize the economy have benefitted some Syrians but left others out. "One can sense their anger," he says. And, of course, exacerbating the problem is the influx of Iraqi refugees—their number had been between 2000 and 4000 a day—who are themselves often in a pitiable state, and whose very presence leads to a shortage of resources and soaring prices. In the fall of 2007, Syria finally closed its borders to all but a handful of Iraqis.

On a potentially positive note, Lebanon and Syria have recently shown signs of political rapprochement. In October 2008, it was announced that the two countries would establish formal diplomatic relations, exchange ambassadors, and attempt the difficult task of delineating the 320-K border that separates them. Implicit in such plans is recognition of Lebanese sovereignty.

In the two and a half years since I returned home, what has *not* changed is my affection for the Syrian people, my gratitude for the opportunity to live among them, and my lively desire to return to Damascus the beautiful.

Evelyn and her partner George Ellenbogen shopping in the souk in Damascus (2005)

III
Think Again

Evelyn on the train to New Mexico

The recurrence of my cancer brought back that long-ago summer when it was first diagnosed. I'd spent the better part of it at Johns Hopkins University, participating in a seminar for college teachers of English. The subject of the seminar was autobiography and confession, genres just beginning to gain a foothold in the academic world. When I applied, I knew my credentials were a bit thin and certainly unorthodox. So far, my only forays into autobiography had been a published essay on *The Prelude* (Wordsworth's long autobiographical poem) and the oral history project I had started on Arab-American women. If I wanted to stretch the point, I could argue that my dissertation on D.H. Lawrence's poetry also qualified, since his verse was so explicitly about his own experience. There had to be other applicants with more to show for themselves, I thought. So when the invitation arrived from Hopkins, I was relieved and glad.

On my first full day in Baltimore, I registered at the college and then walked to the edge of the campus to catch a bus that would take me to my sublet. I remember, so clearly, waiting under a tree, on that pleasant June morning, and feeling a stab of that same happiness I had felt on the first morning of my first trip to Lebanon. On both occasions, I was free, one world temporarily behind me, another opening up but not yet entangling me. Still, from the beginning there were omens. Unpleasant things, two in particular, each frightening in its own way. My landlady, whom I had never set eyes on, bursting in on me as I lay in bed and angrily commanding me to leave (her tenant had no right to sublet); and, a day earlier, a dead mouse spread-eagled in my pop-up toaster—I found it when the slice of bread I was inserting met with resistance. The toaster was not mine but it was hardly the moment to argue property rights: I dumped it on the spot, mouse and all. But also what I have to call a happier omen, the fact that the first person I ran into while registering—he was registering, too—was the young man who would help get me through what was to come. My cancer was treated at home, in Boston, but it was in Baltimore that I found it out.

Cancer

First day home, third since my mastectomy. Noon, and I'm lodged before the TV, in my pj's. Door bell. My aunt. A niggardly, tight-fisted word, *aunt*, meting out its thin swipe of meaning. Arabic is open-handed, answers before you ask. Tells you frankly—this is *umti* (my father's sister), or *khali* (my mother's sister), or *mart ummi* (the wife of my father's brother), or *mart khali* (the wife of my mother's brother). I'm convinced that such distinctions matter.

A digression, that? If you like. But I've had a breast chopped off and, behind it, a membrane scraped away. True, 30 years have passed, but breasts don't grow back, and I think I'm entitled to tell my story my way.

Picture it now—me, *mart khali*, Eyewitness News. On the screen, Betty Ford campaigns, lacquered hair like a vise around her temples. Hasn't it sunk in that Gerry has no chance against the peanut farmer? Not after pardoning Nixon. Never you mind, Betty. Another 25 years and Caroline will toast your husband's political courage while Uncle Ted (admitting he was wrong back then) applauds. *Mart khali* giggles.

If she were closer, she'd poke me in the ribs, I swear she would. As it is, she just points at Betty. "Wearing a falsie," she says.

Mart khali means well. Or, rather, she means nothing at all. Already, it's slipped her mind why she's come visiting. Maybe if she were *khalti*, blood kin, it would stay with her longer. I know her. What's on her mind is her own bosom, of which she's proud as can be. "Help yourself," she'd once said to me, her hands plumping up her boobs. "I've got plenty."

Nineteen seventy-six. The year I found out people are funny.

A friend takes me in. Aside from family, Carol is as close to me as anyone, her home a plausible harbor to steer for. Not that I make it easy for her to say no. My plea: "On short notice, no place else to go." Not literally true, I have a mother in the city. But the worry in her eyes, hour after hour, brings on more guilt than I can manage. "At her age," I keep saying to myself. "At her age." I should be running her errands, driving her to the doctor, telling her laugh-out-loud stories. Not inflicting on her this thing that she can't name in front of me. I wake up that first morning to find Carol in the living room, cigarette in one hand, coffee mug in the other. On the end table beside her, an empty shot glass from the night before. I wait for a sentence out of her mouth, one with the key word *coffee* or—I should be so lucky—*breakfast*. When no offer is forthcoming, I'm reduced to asking. (It goes against the grain. Arabs like to be coaxed. They're not brought up to beg.) "You can look in the fridge," Carol says as if *kitchen* is exotic terrain she knows about only from the pages of the *National Geographic*. The next day, she hurries in the house with a small shopping bag from Filene's Basement. "Look what I bought." For an instant, I think she means for me. She pulls out a saucy red bra and dangles it in front of me, and then a sexy black one. "Isn't it beautiful!" she says as she slips her arms through the straps.

Carol's in love. A nice enough fellow, he seems, but—if you ask me—a bit risky. Before Carol, his only romance—16 years—was with a man. She's out every night, comes back late or not till morning. I cry myself to sleep. We barely see each other, we never talk. Until she delivers an ultimatum. Leave. Months later, her wedding invitation comes in the mail. One of the few moments in my life when I've known exactly what to do: shred the invitation, scatter the pieces in the trash.

The much-vaunted kindness of strangers, that's another thing. In the hospital—backtracking now—I share a room with a woman who has few visitors but many feverish conversations on the phone. I hear enough to know she's disappointed with the world and even less happy with her husband. For sure, she doesn't want to talk to me. Until the night before I'm discharged, when she pulls out a story she's been saving up. Situation: her friend had breast cancer. Rising action: it spread to the brain. Resolution: she's dead. Thank you, unhappy woman in the next bed, thank you for that.

Bicentennial. That was the year. Not all of it bad.

I celebrate the Fourth on the Washington Mall with a young man I am falling for hard. By now, I've found the lump, size of an egg but not yet biopsied. (When you're away from home, as I am, things can move slowly.) So there's room for hope. And for immense anxiety. Stretched out on the lawn, we listen to Sousa marches and the *1812 Overture*, watch the virtuoso leap and fall of fireworks, can't stop smiling. We've cheated fate, by which I mean only that we've made it from Baltimore despite breaking down on the highway with a flat. "Oh, an adventure!" I'd cried out—lighting, for once, on the right thing to say—and seen him relax. Now, in the dark, I lean up against him for comfort and for the pleasure of touching. On the way back to the car I reach for his hand, but his mood has shifted, he keeps his distance. He's come to Baltimore for an eight-week seminar at Hopkins, as have I. His wife waits at the other end of the country.

The biopsy is performed under local anesthetic. No pain, just a tugging at my skin as they stitch me up at the end. "It's a cyst," the surgeon tells me. "Oh, that's good." But he excises a tiny bit of tissue that interests him. I'm to get dressed and take a seat in the waiting room while he studies it under a microscope. I'm not worried, I've had cysts before. Minutes later, he appears in the doorway.

"Sorry, the sample tested positive."

"You mean malignant?"

"You can have reconstructive surgery."

One clipped sentence, another, and he's out of there. Well, of course. I'm not really his patient, he'll never see me again.

Next, a phone call to my GP in Boston, who refuses to take in my news. As if I'm playing an April Fool's joke in July or have fallen for the scare tactics of a charlatan. "But this is Johns Hopkins Hospital," I argue. He allows I have a point and promises a referral to Mass General. I don't phone the man I've been involved with for two years. Days earlier I'd filled him in and asked him to come down. He'd begged off, was on his way to Nantucket Island. "With a woman?" He didn't say no.

Twenty-four hours after the biopsy, I'm back in Boston. On a high. Fresh off the only night I'll ever spend with my young man. I know (because he says so) that he'll tell his wife. "I wish you wouldn't," I say, afraid he'll make me out a charity case: "She was so scared, it was the human thing to do." He won't tell her that he'd laid claim to me— "You're mine for the duration"—days before the diagnosis.

I wind up with the oncologist from hell. Our appointments are regularly scheduled for early afternoon, but he lingers over lunch (drinks too, I'm convinced) with friends. Sometimes they walk him back to his office suite where I sit, trying to distract myself with dated copies of *Good Housekeeping* and *Time*. Already half an hour late, he ushers his pals through the waiting room without a glance at me. They close his office door, and then I hear them laugh. Once he gives me a prescription for the wrong chemo pill. When I unscrew the cap and break the seal, I see the color is off, the shape is wrong. Next appointment, he grunts and scrawls a new prescription. I think but don't dare come out with "Shouldn't you be saying, *Sorry*? Matter of fact, shouldn't you be reimbursing me?" Before I leave, he soils the air: "If anyone sues me, I'm going to quit."

That's the least of it. I remember the day he opines that one person's life or death is not of much account—look at the masses done in by war or natural catastrophe. And I'm supposed to take that how? Another day, and he announces, "I think your cancer will come back." My heart sinks. New test results? He shakes his head. "Gut feeling," he says.

I'd just turned 38. Young for cancer but not for screaming bloody hell when someone mugs me, not for kicking out when someone knocks me flat. I wish I had.

My first visit with the surgeon. My first question: How did this happen? "I had a mammogram," I point out, "a few months ago." I want him to understand that I've played by the rules. I want him to see the unfairness. He knows all about the mammogram, has looked at the images. "They don't show anything suspicious," he says, but he's not surprised. Why is that? He doesn't beat around the bush. "Their equipment at that hospital," he tells me, "is outdated." Think of it. Surely, the staff—the doctors, the technicians—knew about the shortcomings of their radiology department. Surely, my GP, who practices at that hospital and referred me to it for my mammogram, also knew. Yet there they all were, presumably with fingers crossed, assuring me I was fine. Me and how many other women?

I was lucky. If the cyst hadn't clamored for attention, the evil cells lurking underneath might never have been found in time. My lymph nodes—16, I think—all test negative. The surgeon tells me so him-self—he's pleased. (Though, in this business there are no promises.) And—let's add this to the accounting—if I had to have the cancer, at least I also had the romance. On days when I could almost taste death, attraction—already robust—fed off terror.

Evelyn Shakir

ANOTHER WOMAN

It never occurred to me—and I still cannot imagine it—to launch a campaign to capture my young man, break up his marriage, or (consolation prize) angle for a yearly rendezvous. Another woman would not have been deterred by his declaration that he loved his wife. But I—I took it at face value, found solace in the exquisite letters he wrote those first few days when I was back in Boston and in remembering his other declaration: if he'd met me first, I would have been the one. I don't know that it was scruple that choked off romantic fantasy or stayed my hand. Maybe just the conviction that I couldn't compete or that I shouldn't be greedy. Or that what we'd lived through together was a little masterpiece framed and hung now in my memory. Any embellishment, superfluous. But I can imagine another woman who would have battled for the man, her need the only rationale she needed.

I think of Irene. She met my cousin Willy when the company he'd hired on with sent him to its Midwest branch for seasoning. Over the months, they fell in love, or started to. Then, internship over, he returned to his family's home in Boston. Letters and long-distance phone calls followed, but who knows? Maybe she sensed a cooling, a pulling back. She quit her job, hopped a plane, and showed up on his family's doorstep. No choice, they had to take this stranger in. That's where Arab hospitality proved her friend. Soon she saw (if she hadn't known it earlier) that, in this household, her Catholicism was a strike against her, as was her bold dash to the Eastern seaboard. Not well brought up, my aunt and uncle must have thought. She waited them out, and their hesitations. She and Willy married. If she'd been in my place, I don't know what she would have done about my young man, but I'm betting she'd have tried something.

I wonder. Which is to say that I am both curious and amazed. Are we programmed differently at birth? Or is it the alcoholic father, the pious mother, the illiterate grandparents that lay down the template of our character? And, in the process, spell out our destiny.

158

So, no, it did not occur to me to complicate that young man's life. What did occur to me—a few years before cancer struck—was a different sort of plan, entirely: to get myself overseas. With my Ph.D. almost in hand, I wrote to the chair of the English Department at the American University of Beirut, asking about the prospect of a job. "Why do you want to go there?" my advisor asked. "How will that help your career?" Today I know that it would have done just fine by my career. My advisor, brilliant as he was, didn't get it, that the new focus on things international and intercultural was more than a fad, that there was gold in them thar foreign hills. He didn't have a clue that AUB, established by American missionaries in the 19th century, was the most celebrated university in the Middle East and bordering lands, the alma mater of princes, kings, and presidents. It's a sure bet, he would have had no notion of where to look for Lebanon on a map. The Beirut of bombed out buildings, blood-spattered streets, feral militias, and butchered civilians—which would teach Americans a new piece of geography—was still five years away.

But what continues to astonish is not my advisor's miscalculation of the path toward professional advancement, but rather that career was all he cared about. "So what?" I want to say to him now. "The hell with plotting out, step-by-cautious-step, a route to tenure. I was young, adventure called, blood called. Lebanon was the country my parents came from, it was where Jesus went to a wedding in Cana, where the Romans built a magnificent temple to Jupiter/Baal, where the River Ibrahim runs red in the spring with the blood of Adonis, where cedars were felled to build Solomon's temple at Jerusalem, where a gem of a Crusader castle still sits by the sea. Novelty, if nothing else, would nurture mind and spirit. I would become fluent in my parents' tongue."

The chair at AUB wrote back. American himself, he was eager to recruit Lebanese who lived overseas. No full-time teaching slot was open, but, if I wanted, he would try to cobble together a package which would have me teach a course or two and spend the rest of my time advising female undergraduates. I diddled, I had second thoughts, it was so far away, my advisor was cool to the idea, my mother was almost 80. By the time I typed up my little note—"Well, yes, that would be very nice"—it was too late. Another woman would have answered the chair by return mail or transoceanic telephone. Whatever it took to nail the offer down before it slithered away. This time—no two ways about it—we are talking regret.

DREAMS

After my diagnosis, I go into deep sleeps and wake with scraps of dream pasted, like tattered posters, to my brain. In one, I look down at my hand, at the ring I've hardly taken off in years. One of its twin amethysts is gone. My unconscious, not subtle, settles for the easy visual pun. I've always been a dreamer—in the literal sense. Anxiety the medium in which my dreaming flourishes. The night before my Ph.D. oral exams, I dream that a doctor is examining me. "Where's my hand now?" he keeps asking as he lifts and lowers it behind my back. My answer, always the same: "It's over my head, it's over my head." As I said, not subtle. One of my more intricate dreams, also from my graduate school years, must have been prompted by anger, but at whom I do not remember. I am sitting in a darkened movie theater; on the screen a line-up of cheerleaders are going through their paces for an "Adam University." As they swing their arms down hard in unison, half the screen goes black, and, at the same instant, their cheer is truncated, front and back. "Dam U," the cheerleaders yell, "Damn you!"

In the cancer dream I best remember, I'm on a flowery hillside. It's summer, but snow is falling. Untimely blight. Easy to interpret that one. A bottle of perfume, labeled "My Joy," figures prominently though I no longer remember exactly how. It doesn't matter, what counts is this: my unconscious, the imp, has collapsed, into one, two scents widely advertised back then—"Joy" by Jean Patou, and Lanvin's "My Sin." Joy and sin, one and the same. In the context of the dream, the point seems clear enough. You fool around, you pay the price. Voices from our childhood dog us into adulthood, voices that tell us we are naughty, that we are bad. No matter how we run, we are never out of earshot.

Evelyn at Rowlandson Rock, Lancaster (2009)

Evelyn at a book signing for *Bint Arab*

Why I Write

Whatever's on your mind, forget it. I don't have time.

Not at 60, with a lifetime's picking-up to do. The spare bedroom already metamorphosed into a storeroom (junkyard really) that's off limits to the cleaning lady because there are no clear surfaces left to dust or mop. Clutter is an army on the march, swarming now through my own bedroom door. Floor giving ground to catalogues from Crate and Barrel and Pottery Barn, newsletters on women's health, weeks of the *New Yorker*, Amtrak commuter schedules, utility bills, to-do lists; scribbled recipes from a TV chef; crosswords—acrostic and diagramless—torn from the *Times*, solicitations that I just might answer, medical bills that need phoning in about since my internist's office never gets it right. Where have all the copayments gone?

When the cleaning lady is due, I make my bed and stack the stuff on it, together with piles of sweaters, T-shirts, jeans, out-of -season skirts, and fabric destined to be curtains when my sewing machine is finally up and running. Or when I buy a new one. It's hopeless, desktop and desk drawers cry for mercy. Shelves bulge obscenely. My bedroom closet closes in on itself like a wound intent on healing. My dresser is a toy, a child's dresser I bought my first year in graduate school when what did it matter and who could afford?

Lately, I haven't bothered sweeping the stuff back off my bed after the cleaning woman has had her way. Let it be. At night, I drop a pillow on the floor, spread out sheets and blanket and camp out. When I wake now in the morning, my muscles don't ache the way they used to. And they used to because the mattress on my bed is old and sags. I have to buy a new one. It's on my list of things to do. Together with essays to grade, spring bulbs to plant, a bone-density test to schedule, an aunt to visit, bank statements to balance, bills to pay, old clothes to put out for the Salvation Army. Sewing machine to get up and running. Unless I buy a new one.

Is everyone like this?

Is anyone like this?

Well, yes. I have a friend. She lives in a nifty Manhattan apartment with a doorman. Fancy moldings, a large entryway. Antique furniture shipped north that she inherited from her mother, oil portraits of ancestors in gilt frames. The only way to navigate the living room is by a narrow lane that meanders from doorway at one end to desk at the other. A swath mown through a field thick with armloads of manila folders. They mound like stacks of hay. "Molly of the Piles," my brother calls her. Behind the door, her bike.

Like me, Molly has a woman who comes in every other week. Where does she step? What does she clean? The tub and toilet, I guess. Every other surface burdened with letters, paperbacks, and playbills; pewter candlesticks, bicycle helmet, and running shoes. Floor, tables, sofa, all function now as shelves. Chairs also, except for two rockers, the one she curls up in after supper and the cat's. Den and even bath are much the same. Bedroom, too—one side of her double bed out of commission. Clothes hang from the lintel of every door. She can't have people in for dinner or to schmooze. Dates leave her in the lobby. I wonder if that's the point. Molly, is this a chastity belt we have here?

Or something else? Her father, a dashing officer—I've seen his picture—died in a prisoner-of-war camp in the Pacific. She was a toddler. When she was 25, her mother died of cancer. Against the greedy fates that pounce and snatch, is she just hanging on to what she can?

But, oh, she goes too far. Each time I phone from Boston, the machine picks up. Surely, she must sometimes be at home—morning, evening, Wednesday, Sunday, sunny day, snowy day, holiday. She prefers to let the messages pile up.

If opposites attract, have I got a guy for Molly! Roscoe is a man I teach with. Once, already in the neighborhood, I dropped by his condo to return a book I'd borrowed from his office. He made me take my shoes off before I crossed the threshold and slip into slippers he had ready at the door. "Hardwood floors," his explanation. Inside, I looked around for what was missing. To my left, the galley kitchen, counters bare, dishes, pots, and pans all stowed away. Through another open door, the bedroom, but I could see that wasn't where he kept his junk. Cagily, I admired an antique wardrobe in the hallway, and he opened it. Shelves of sweaters neatly folded and exactly spaced— a checkerboard of argyles and Alpine patterns.

It takes decision to create such order. No smudgy thinking, no tangles of *what if* or *on the other hand*. Roscoe knows where things go. Roscoe knows right from wrong. Hear him hold forth on the Middle East, big business, or the pedagogy of freshman composition.

I perch on a leather chair in his living room (immaculate too, of course). Negative space defined by everything not there. No stray keys or pencils or loose coins scattered about, no CD jackets or empty coffee cups. No books splayed on the coffee table, no newspaper. And yet he reads. "Your apartment is beautiful," I said. He looked around with satisfaction. Pointed out the touch of red in a sofa pillow that repeated the red of a vase by the window. "A room should be like a poem," he told me. "Nothing superfluous, everything converging." I went home discouraged and ashamed.

Still, the public rooms in my house—living room, dining room, and even kitchen—are, by sane standards, presentable enough. The face I show the world. Upstairs, behind closed doors, it's quite another story. Upstairs and down—sounds like the makings of an inverted allegory. My mother didn't fool with such hocus-pocus. She just told me I was lazy.

What would she say if she knew that, eight years after her death, her bedroom is still as she left it? A skirt on the sewing machine, waiting to be mended. Underthings in a hamper. Nylons bunched in her everyday shoes by the bed. She and my brother shared that house, and he still lives there. But, of course, he'd never think of sorting through or putting things to right. Woman's work, he tells me. I guess he's right.

But I don't know that he's impatient with my procrastination. In fact, I think he's glad. It's useful to have something on me when I'm after him to pull himself together, do this, do that. "Before I'm senile," I tell him, "and won't know the difference." Or else I say, "Before I die."

"Mama's room," he answers.

So I've been thinking. (Mama's room aside because surely that's a special case.) When it comes to getting off the fence—let's say, making up my mind to give up on the old Singer—I'm like Bartleby the Scrivener, *I would prefer not to*. What if I jump the wrong way? "Not every choice is a test," my friend lectures me. "No one is grading you." But it's not just fear of failure that stymies me. My astronomical sign is Cancer, and, like the crab, I have trouble letting go. The old sewing machine once belonged to my mother, she sewed my dresses on it all through elementary and even into graduate school; the mini-skirt at the back of the closet reminds me of when I wore my hair in a shag and men (of some discernment, let me add) told me I was beautiful; the overflow of books are ones I once annotated with exclamation points in the margins—back when I thought I could discover truth.

And sometimes choice—keep the dress or throw it out, order the lamp or junk the catalogue—is not the issue. I will pay the electric bill, ignoring it is not an option; I will grade the essays, much as I might like to dump them in a barrel and light a match; I will even schedule that bone-density test, because I remember a friend's mother whose osteoporosis was so bad, bones broke when she was transferred from bed to stretcher. I will. But, meanwhile, here I am, nursing this reluctance to move when I can sit; to speak when I can keep mum; to go out when I can stay in; to make a foot of progress instead of lovely, detailed lists. *Lazy as the day is long*, my mother said.

Naturally, I have other theories.

Theory A: I learned early that action is perilous, it leads to tears.

Like pushing your girlfriend for fun—she trips on her father's favorite LP and breaks it; or saying a word you didn't know was bad—your grandmother slaps you. Or when he's pushed you too far, biting your brother's finger and watching blood collect. Sometimes the harder you try to be careful, the worse things turn out. One childhood day my father gave me a dollar bill for an errand to the store and, for my reward, a Hershey bar. I couldn't wait, I had to eat in on the way. In a fit of virtue—at school, the principal had lectured us on littering—I tore the wrapper off, stooped, and threw it down the sewer grate. But when I opened my palm, the wrapper was still there. I went crying home, my father got out his fishing pole, the boy next door stood over him to watch. Only a dollar, but a dollar was a lot.

That's one read. Lie low; the less you do, the safer.

Theory B: I learned early that action is futile. It doesn't get you anywhere.

Of course, human nature being what it is, there are days when I forget. For instance, I eye a table that I've inherited (though that word's too fancy). It's in ratty shape. But I can go to the hardware store, can't I? I can ask the man there what stuff to buy and what to do to make it beautiful again. It's May, the month that makes me feel all things are possible.

I procrastinate. Weeks pass. By the Fourth of July, the spell is broken. I see I'm foolish to dream I can play fairy godmother to this piece of furniture, my skills don't lie in that direction. And, anyway, this Cinderella is too far gone. Rickety, scratched, dirt-dark, inlay peeled off from when we were kids and couldn't keep from worrying it with sharp fingernails.

Granted, in its day the table was nice enough, two feet, some inches square with alabaster petals and delicate legs that curve. Reminiscent of the old country, it was a wedding present to my parents.

To say that it deteriorated as their marriage did would be too easy. But there's no denying that we children were hard on both. My father too old and too short-tempered to cope with a son and daughter who made noise or had ideas. My mother, older too. In her forties when I was born (my father in his fifties) and still ambitious. A business of her own to start and run. Charity work to do. A house to keep. No time for fun. After she retired, her sister-in-law and I watched her one afternoon playing with my cousin's children. My aunt said, "Your mother never played with you when you were little." My aunt, always one to twist the knife.

The raised voices I remember between my parents were all about my brother or, less often, me. Beyond doubt, without us, they would have been less angry and more reconciled to their joint venture. But also more ashamed. Their childless state. I, removed by a generation from the villages they called home, can hardly comprehend the stigma.

As a child, I thought that I could make everything right. If I had enough faith. If I kept my case before God. "Dear Lord," I prayed, kneeling at the window before getting into bed, "make Philip a good boy." I might as well have saved my breath. I tried to be good myself.

Some days I'd come home from school and sponge the kitchen walls with Spic and Span. Other times I'd get out the Brasso and polish the copper water pipes that ran along one wall and up through the ceiling to the bathroom. Always I'd wash the breakfast dishes and make the beds. That was expected. But the walls and pipes were a bravura flourish.

When my mother got home from work, I'd wait for her to notice. And, when she didn't, I'd point out the clean walls or the shiny pipes or the linoleum I'd washed and waxed. "Good," she'd say. But that wasn't enough, not for the effort I'd put in. And then she'd add, "Next time . . ." And I'd hear about another task that needed doing. It was cockeyed. Instead of gaining, I was losing ground.

Sometimes, when my students get discouraged because I've covered their essays with suggestions and corrections, I want to tell them who's to blame. The one who taught me that good is merely fair, and that fair is never good enough.

Theory C. Age has a deadening effect.

With parents the same age as my friends' grandparents, I was always afraid they were on their way out. I'd even make bargains with God. If I'm really good, will you let mama live long enough to watch me walk down the aisle? For her part, she was busy sounding the alarm. *Who knows how much longer I'll be around?*

So many grants and fellowships I never applied for because I'd have to project myself into the future. "Next year," I'd have to say, "I plan to . . ." But I couldn't because next year I'd be a year older and my mother a year closer to her end.

She died when she was 94. I was 52.

When time races in on me in waves, washing over my thighs and surging above my waist, I look around to see how others cope. I watch them plunge headfirst into surf and shoot up in deep water, whipping their hair out of their eyes, propelling themselves forward with long, smooth strokes. Reckless, reckless—so far out now, they can't hear my call. I stay in the shallows, bobbing and swaying in place, toes touching ground. And talk to the air, tell on myself, tell myself stories—middle, beginning, and end.

Evelyn writing in her studio.